BURGESS UNABRIDGED

WOWZE

BURGESS UNABRIDGED

A New Dictionary
of Words you have always Needed

BY GELETT BURGESS
Author of "Goops," "Are You a Bromide?"
"The Maxims of Methuselah," "The
Maxims of Noah," & c.

With a New Foreword by
PAUL DICKSON

Illustrations by
HERB ROTH

Walker & Company
New York

Published by Walker Publishing Company, Inc., New York
Distributed to the trade by Holtzbrinck Publishers

All papers used by Walker & Company are natural, recyclable
products made from wood grown in well-managed forests.
The manufacturing processes conform to the environmental
regulations of the country of origin.

LIBRARY OF CONGRESS CATALOGING-IN-PUBLICATION DATA
HAS BEEN APPLIED FOR

ISBN-10: 0-8027-1646-6
ISBN-13: 978-0-8027-1646-0

Visit Walker & Company's Web site at www.walkerbooks.com

First published 1914 by Frederick A. Stokes Company
Reprinted 1986 with a new foreword by Archon Books,
an imprint of The Shoe String Press
First Walker edition 2007

1 3 5 7 9 10 8 6 4 2

Printed in the United States of America by Quebecor World Fairfield

FOREWORD
by PAUL DICKSON

When Gelett Burgess died in California in 1951 at the age of eighty-five he was accorded a *New York Times* obituary which said that he had spent "sixty of his eighty-five years putting onto paper ideas and words that were to make several generations much happier."[1]

The man worked hard for such an epitaph. Among other things, he was a draughtsman (for the Southern Pacific Railroad); a college instructor (University of California at Berkeley); an editor (beginning with the MIT *Tech* and including three "little" literary magazines); a painter; a builder of nonsense machines; a poet, a playwright, and an author.

Gelett Burgess wrote forty-nine books of which eleven were novels. Some were successful, others not; but all had an aura of derring-do and experiment about them. Today they seem to have the whiff of gunpowder rather than the mere mustiness of old books. It is telling that Burgess's first book, published in 1886, was entitled *Some Experiences With Hashish*.

One gets an idea of what he was up to in this little blurb he wrote about himself:

> "G.B. loves tours-de-force. He loves machinery, and the intricacies of technique. He adores the extravagant, the outrageous. But he used his gift always to demonstrate the absurdities of life. He creates his characters only to destroy them. He formulates complex theories [Bromides and Sulphites?] and blows them up with blasts of laughter. He is amused at everything, respects nothing."

No doubt there was sadness here. Little has been written about him but what has confirms this. A fine doctoral thesis by Joseph

vii

BURGESS UNABRIDGED

Moorehead Backus written shortly after Burgess's death calls his "a life of tragedy disguised as comedy."[2] But part of what Backus saw as tragic was his inability to deal with "adult conceptions" so it may be an overstatement. What he has left us—what can be found in the libraries that don't purge books too easily and in the back rooms of used book stores—is funny and readable and no more tragic than, say, Murphy's Law or Dagwood Bumstead's inability to enjoy an uninterrupted bath. He believed that men and women were vastly different and that there was a battle of the sexes. He was as liable to drop a line which today would be labeled sexist as would James Thurber, Dorothy Parker, Fred Allen, or W.C. Fields.

Burgess wrote so many different things and concerned himself with so much for so long that you could say all sorts of things about him and find that there was at least a moment in his life when any one thing was true. To say that he was an iconoclast is to remind one that he lost his job at the University of California for destroying the campus cast-iron statue of the noted Dr. Cogswell. As the creator and editor of little magazines he went beyond experimental literature even to experiment with paper. The *Lark,* which he helped found in 1895, was printed on thin, yellow bamboo paper he had found in San Francisco's Chinatown and when he started the zany *Le Petit Journal des Refusées* he printed it on sheets of discontinued wallpaper.

Often it was difficult to know if he was being serious or simply poking fun at serious people. In 1910 he staged a one-man show of thirty of his watercolors at a posh Manhattan gallery. It was titled "Experiments in Symbolistic Psychology" and debate soon raged between one faction which saw it as serious and profound and another which argued it was calculated nonsense.

He built all sorts of odd mechanical constructions, spending months on some of them. Recalling his fascination with model building, W.F. Miksch wrote of him in a 1964 article in the humor magazine *For Laughing Out Loud,* "One time he worked for two solid weeks constructing a miniature farmhouse—a remarkable piece of model building right down to its mica windows and green velvet lawn; then exhibiting it at a dinner party, he astonished admiring guests by setting it on fire."[3]

Ironically, Burgess was most noted for a small thing he wrote for the first issue of the *Lark* in 1895:[4]

viii

FOREWORD

> *I never saw a purple cow*
> *I never hope to see one;*
> *But I can tell you anyhow,*
> *I'd rather see than be one.*

It was so popular for such a long time that both Presidents Roosevelt were said to regard it as a pet ditty. He was known as the "Purple Cow" man for so long that he later rebutted it:[5]

> *Ah, yes, I wrote the "Purple Cow,"*
> *I'm Sorry, now, I wrote it;*
> *But I can tell you Anyhow*
> *I'll kill you if you Quote it!*

Its power was such that one morning in 1940—forty-five years after he wrote it—he was summoned from his room in New York's Imperial Hotel by a brash public relations man named Jim Moran. The p.r. man had hold of a purebred Jersey cow which had been dyed purple. "There!" said Moran, "Now you've seen one."[6]

Another Burgess creation were boneless, ill-mannered figures called Goops. He created them for children and they were used to undermine bad manners.[7]

> *The Goops, they lick their fingers,*
> *And the Goops, they lick their knives.*
> *They spill their broth on the tablecloth—*
> *Oh, they lead disgusting lives!*

> *The Goops, they talk while eating,*
> *And loud and fast they chew.*
> *So that is why I'm glad that I*
> *Am not a Goop—are you?*

Burgess Unabridged came out in 1914 and was, according to biographer Backus, "ill-timed." As he explains, "With its commendation of both Theodore Roosevelt and the Kaiser Wilhelm as having 'spuzz', it appeared in September, 1914, shortly after the Battle of the Marne and before the German occupation of Antwerp." For their part, the critics were only able to muster faint praise for the book although the *Times*[8] of London did call it a "feat of ingenuity." Others found it a bit too unorthodox and the best the *New York Times* could say of it was that it would amuse those "who have a liking for Burgess humor."[9]

The book had a short bookstore shelf life and sold less than 4,000 copies. Until now, seventy-two years later, the book has not been reprinted and has become a true rarity. It is only in the collections of a few large libraries and it seldom shows up in the used book market.

Yet for all of that, its influence has and still is being felt. Its neologisms show up in all sorts of places and to this day are trotted out when the point is being made that the English language is flexible and hungry for new words. Burgess, along with Lewis Carroll and Edward Lear, always seems to come up at this time.

After *Burgess Unabridged* was published it became an inspiration for those who dared play with and create new words. The words themselves can still draw a crowd; for instance, Russell Baker devoted his whole column for August 30, 1981 to Burgess's own meaning for the word, *wog*. This word was and is an ugly racial slur, but one can see Burgess at work playfully giving it a new and humorous meaning. Essentially, Burgess's humor was benign and one imagines that he would have found the other meaning offensive.

One of the words which underscores Burgess's remarkable linguistic touch is not in this book: *bromide*. In April 1906, Burgess published an article in *The Smart Set* (the magazine which was later to become much more famous when H. L. Mencken and George Jean Nathan became its coeditors.) The article entitled "The Sulphitic Theory, or Are You a Bromide?" said that all people are easily divided into two groups, or families: Sulphites and Bromides.

"The Bromide does its thinking by syndication," wrote Burgess. "They have their hair cut every month and their minds keep regular office hours."

"The accepted Bromidic belief is that each of the ordinary acts of life is, and necessarily must be, accompanied by its own especial remark or opinion." Burgess listed dozens of Bromidic sayings or "bromidioms": "I don't know much about art, but I know what I like"; "It isn't the money—it's the principle of the thing"; and "Of course, if you happen to want a policeman, there's never one within miles of you."

On the other hand, Sulphites do their own thinking and "are agreed upon most of the basic facts of life, and this common understanding makes it possible for them to eliminate the obvious from their conversation."[10]

The article made an immediate splash. Writing about it during 1955 in the *Baltimore Sun* Louis Graves said, "I was a reporter in New York then and I remember how joyfully the article was acclaimed by the intellectuals (which term I am now stretching to embrace not only scholars, novelists, essayists, poets, dramatists, and editors, but also writers of all ranks). The intellectuals talked and wrote so much about the article that they made its subject familiar to almost everybody who was able to read."[11]

A year later the article was beefed up into a small book entitled *Are You a Bromide?* It went into many editions and could still be bought in larger bookstores a decade later.

The word *bromide*—in the sense of a flat, trite, commonplace statement—had soon become part of the language. It was not exactly as Burgess had intended it, as he had meant *bromide* as a personality type and *bromidiom* as the kind of statement made by such a person. But it was Burgess at work and by 1920 people were using it to mean any "trite remark."[12] One could fill fat scrapbooks with examples of its use in print ("The old bromide that poetry never sells is once again proved to be wrong," for example, from *Publisher's Weekly*).

Blurb, which Burgess created in 1907 and which he used in this book (page 7) is an even stronger refutation of the bromide, "You just can't go out and make up a word and expect it to become part of the English language." *Blurb* is now more firmly a part of the language than it was anytime during Burgess's lifetime and no writer worth his or her sodium writes a book without dreaming of the blurbs that Norman Mailer and Kurt Vonnegut will write for it. It now seems to be coming into its own as a verb, at least in New York where I heard an editor say that "Peter Drucker hadn't blurbed another writer in years."

It would be hard to say that this book is anything more or less than what it is: a gleeful, linguistic romp for people who believe, like Burgess, that G supplies more *spuzz* to a word than can be obtained from any other letter. It is also a rarity as a work of humor written before World War I that is still fresh and funny. The clichéd response for something that still works well after this many years is to brand it a classic and be done with it. But classic is the wrong word. It reeks of *nink* and *ovotch* with overtones of *snosh*. Verbal *voip*, if you will, which too many will quickly *machizzle*. And, at its worst and most tortured, *flooijab*.

1. *New York Times,* 20 Sept. 1951, p. 30, col. 4.
2. Joseph Moorehead Backus, *A Biography of the Man Who Wrote the Purple Cow* (Ph.D. diss., University of California, 1961), available in microfilm.
3. W.F. Miksch, "At Last He Saw a Purple Cow," *For Laughing Out Loud* 30, (March 1964): p. 26.
4. This appears in many collections and anthologies. One of the more recent of these is *The Purple Cow and Other Poems* by Gelett Burgess published in 1968 by The Henry E. Huntington Library, San Marino, California.
5. Quoted widely, it appears in James Thorpe's introduction to the aforementioned Huntington Library edition.
6. Related in the Miksch article.
7. Gelett Burgess, *Goops and how to be them* (New York: Frederick A. Stokes, 1900). Reprinted by Dover Books, 1962.
8. *London Times,* 29 October 1914, p. 483.
9. *New York Times,* 4 October 1914, p. 419:3.
10. Gelett Burgess, "Are you a bromide?", *The Smart Set,* (April 1906).
11. *Baltimore Sun,* 29 August 1955, p. 19.
12. Stuart Berg Flexner, *I Hear America Talking* (New York: Von Nostrand, 1976), p. 65.

INTRODUCTION

Yes, I have written a dictionary. Worcester and Webster are all right in their way, and Stormuth will do very well for Englishmen — but they're not up to date. Mrs. Century's book is a bit better and even old Dr. Standard's Compendium of Useful Information includes my own words, " bromide " and " sulphite." It's good enough for last year, but " Burgess Unabridged " will give the diction of the year 1915.

For, the fact is, English is a growing language, and we have to let out the tucks so often, that no last season's model will ever fit it. English isn't like French, which is corseted and gloved and clad and shod and hatted strictly according to the rules of the Immortals. We have no Academy, thank Heaven, to tell what is real English and what isn't. Our Grand Jury is that ubiquitous person, Usage, and we keep him pretty busy at his job. He's a Progressive and what he likes, he'll have, in spite of lexicographers, college professors and authors of " His Complete Works." That's the reason why English has ousted Volapük and Esperanto as a world language. It snuggles right down where you live and makes itself at home.

How does English shape itself so comfortably to the body of our thought? With a new wrinkle here and a little more breadth there, with fancy trimmings, new styles, fresh materials and a genius for adapting itself to all sorts of wear. Everybody is working at it, tailoring it, fitting it, decorating it. There is no person so humble but that he can suggest an improvement that may easily become the reigning mode.

Slang, I once defined as " The illegitimate sister of Poetry " — but slang is sometimes better than that; it often succeeds in marrying the King's English, and at that ceremony there are dozens of guests. There's the poker player, who contributes for his wedding present, "The limit" and "Make good" and "Four flush." Politics hands over "Boodle," "Mugwump" and "Gerrymander." The thief presents his "Jimmy," "Doss," "Kip," "Heeler," "Split," "Lag," "Swag" and "Dope." The horse race gives us "Neck and neck"; baseball, "Putting one over." Even the baby offers "Goo-goo." Illustrations, however, are boring.

But slang, strictly, consists in the adaptation of phrases; it does not often — not often enough at any rate — coin new words. Thieves' patter or jargon or cant provides us almost with a language of itself, and words from the Underworld are continually being added to the language. Like the turkey trot, "We first endure, then pity, then embrace." So from all sources the language recruits new phrases, new expressions, even new rules of grammar. Horrible as they are to the conservative, common usage accepts them and they become classic. Professor Lounsbury of Yale is kept busy justifying them. He, alone of all grammarians, sees that the split infinitive must come, that verbs must be constructed of nouns. He recognizes the new function of the potential mood, in "I should worry" and "Wouldn't that jar you?"

Yes, it's easy enough to coin a phrase, to adapt an old word to a new use, like "Chestnut" and "Lemon" and "Peach." It's easy to abbreviate words, like "Gent" and "Pants" and "Exam" and "Phone" and "Stylo." It's easier still to fill the new dictionary with new derivatives from Latin or Greek or crowd in French. The scientific word requires a little invention. "Radioactive" and "Aileron" and "Hypofenyl-tribrompropionic" need only a scholastic delving in ancient tongues. But to invent a new word right out of the air or the cigarette smoke is another thing. And that's what I determined to do.

Yes, I know it has been tried, but it's never been seriously and deliberately gone about. It has been haphazard work, the result of a mere accident, or vaudeville high spirits. But the way such neologisms have become quickly current shows that here's a field for high endeavor, and a little success with

INTRODUCTION

" Blurb " and " Goop " encourage me to proceed in the good work. We need so many new words, and we need 'em quick. The question is: How to get 'em?

Of course, we might ransack the back numbers of the language and dig up archaic words. Many such have been dropped from the original Anglo-Saxon. There is " Dindle," to shake, and " Foin " to thrust, and " Gree " and " Lusk " and " Sweven." But the need for most of them has long gone by. We do not " Feutre " our spears, because we have no spears to feutre. We carry no " Glaive," we wear no " Coif."

So with the bright gems of Elizabethan diction. A " Bonnibel " is now a nectarine. To " Brabble " is now to " Chew the rag." What is a " Scroyle "? — a " Cad," a " Bad Actor "? A " Gargrism " has become " A Scream." So the old names become mere poetic decorations. Why, the word " Fro " we dare use only in a single collocation! And as for " Welkin," " Lush," and " Bosky "— who dares to lead their metric feet into the prim paths of prose? Let bygones be bygones. Look elsewhere.

Samoa has an ideal language, and there it was I got my inspiration. Can't we make English as subtle as Samoan? I wondered. There they have a single word, meaning, " A-party-is-approaching-which-contains-neither-a-clever-man-nor-a-pretty-woman." Another beautiful word describes " A-man-who-climbs-out-on-the-limbs-of-his-own-breadfruit-tree-to-steal-the-breadfruit-of-his-neighbor." "*Suiia*" means "Change-the-subject-you-are-on-dangerous-ground." Another happy word expresses a familiar situation —" To-look-on-owl-eyed-while-others-are-getting-gifts." Have we anything in English as charmingly tactful as this? No, our tongue is almost as crude as pidjin-English itself, where piano is " Box-you-fight-him-cry."

But the time has come for a more scientific attempt to enlarge the language. The needs of the hour are multifarious and all unfilled. There are a thousand sensations that we can describe only by laborious phrases or metaphors, a thousand characters and circumstances, familiar to all, which shriek for description.

It has, of course, been tried before. Think what a success the scheme was when it was so long ago attempted. The first Nonsense Book containing really new words was published in 1846 by Edward Lear, but he failed to appreciate his opportunity. Of all his names, the " Jumblies " alone survive. Lewis Carroll later went about it more deliberately. His immortal poem, " Jabberwocky," has become a classic; but even in that masterpiece, how many words are adapted to modern use? " Slithy " perhaps and " Chortle "— though no one has ever been able to pronounce it properly to this day. Oh yes, "Galumph," I forgot that. Not even " The Hunting of the Snark " has made the title rôle popular amongst bromides. Why? His fatal rule was, " Take care of the sounds and the sense will take care of itself."

A dozen years ago a little girl tried it with fair success. In her " Animal Land, where there are no People," however, I can find no word I have ever heard used outside its covers, no word like " Hoodlum," or " Flunk " or " Primp," " Quiz," "Cabal " or " Fad " or " Fake."

The thing must be done, and so I did it. Slang is sporadic; its invention is crude and loose. It is a hit-or-miss method, without direction or philosophy. Our task is serious; we must make one word blossom where a dozen grew before. A myriad necessities urge us. I found myself often confronted with an idea which baffled me and forced me to talk gibberish. How, for instance, can one describe the appearance of an elderly female in plush dancing a too conscientious tango? How do *you*, gentle reader, portray your emotion when, on a stormy night, as you stand on the corner the trolley-car whizzes by and fails to stop for you? Where is the word that paints the mild, faint enjoyment of a family dinner with your wife's relations?

You see how inarticulate you are, now, don't you, when a social emergency arises? — when you want to give swift tongue to your emotions? What can you say when you're jilted? — how mention the feeling of a broken finger-nail on satin — your esthetic delight in green-trading-stamp furniture? How do you feel with a person whose name you cannot quite remember? Why, we need at least a gross of assorted nouns this very day! What is the name of a business enterprise that was born dead? What do you call the woman who telephones to you during business hours? What is a woman who wears dirty white gloves? What is a man who gives you advice " for your own good "? Well, behold a guide to help you; — read " Burgess Unabridged." It is the dictionary of the Futurist language!

Yes, my modest " Unabridged " will " fill a long felt want." It will solidify the chinks of conversation, express the inexpressible, make our English language ornamental, elegant, distinguished, accurate. Other dictionaries have recorded the words of yesterday, my lexicon will give the words of tomorrow. What matter if none of them is " derived from two Greek words "? My words will be imaginotions, penandinkumpoops, whimpusles, mere boojums rather than classic snarks, for I shall not construct " Portmanteau " words, like Lewis Carroll. I shall create them from instinctive, inarticulate emotions, hot from the depths of necessity. No " Onomatopœia," either, for I do not hold with those who say that the origin of language is in the mere mimicry of natural sounds. No, like the intense poetic pre-Raphaelite female, who says and feels that her soul is violet, when I see a hand-embroidered necktie, I dive deep in my inner consciousness and bring up, writhing in my hand, the glad word, " Gorgule," or " Golobrifaction " or " Diabob."

For, as my friend, the Reverend Edward P. Foster, A.M., of Marietta, Ohio, has pointed out, in his great work on Ro, the *a priori* method is the only rational principle upon which to coin new words. Volapük, Esperanto, Idiom Neutral, Interlingua and Ido all have fallen by the wayside of this " philosophical " route. It is as futile to try to make the sound suggest the sense. For, investigation will show that so many senses are suggested that the word lacks definition.

Not only does "stave" seem to imply a barrel, but music. And, if you take the sound alone, we have such different meanings as wright, right, write and rite, not to speak of exactly opposite interpretations in such word as "cleave."

What Ro, therefore, attempts so ambitiously, I do in a more humble spirit, contenting myself with the manufacture of words to explain some of the more subtle relationships and exigencies of civilized life. I confess the work is, to a great extent, subjective and personal. I have but ministered to my own direst needs.

So contriving, choosing my words from some vague sense of color, mood, an instinctive feeling of appropriateness, I trust that I have not made my method monotonous. I must confess, however, that in my experimentation, certain sounds appealed more strongly than others to my comic spirit. The frequent use of the "oo" will perhaps require an apology, and the almost equally merry "aw." The other "long" vowels, such as "ee" and "ay" and "o" seemed inadequate to my use. Of consonants, my "G" is, no doubt, most frequent. "G" supplies spuzz to a word that can hardly be obtained elsewhere in the alphabet. "K" also has a bite, but it is frequently too suggestive for our delicate susceptibilities. "L"—what could one do in such a work, without the gentle liquid that euphonizes the most savage of consonants! Also I confess having fallen in love with the anapest.

And yet, many of these words will not, at first sound, seem appropriate. Let me remind you of Mr. Oliver Herford's not too original discovery (most children make it earlier), than any word, when often repeated, becomes strange and barbaric, even as his favorite "looking-glass" after being pronounced several times, grows marvellously beautiful and romantic.

So, as a corollary to this principle, you will, I hope, find that even my fierce and uncouth syllables may, when iterated, grow less unusual, strangely familiar, even; and, little by little, as their sharp corners and edges are worn smooth by use, they will fit into your conversation and nestle into place, making your talk firmer, more expressive and wonderfully adequate to your daily needs.

> *When vorianders seek to huzzlecoo,*
> * When jurpid splooch or vilpous drillig bores,*
> *When cowcats kipe, or moobles wog, or you*
> * Machizzled are by yowfs or xenogores,*
>
> *Remember Burgess Unabridged, and think,*
> * How quisty is his culpid yod and yab!*
> *No fidgeltick, with goigsome iobink,*
> * No varmic orobaldity — his gab!*
>
> *No more tintiddling slubs, like fidgelticks,*
> * Rizgidgeting your speech, shall lallify;*
> *But your jujasm, like vorgid gollohix,*
> * Shall all your woxy meem golobrify!*

GELETT BURGESS.

New York, June 1st, 1914.

BURGESS ABRIDGED:

100 CHOICE SELECTIONS

1. **Agowilt.** Sickening terror, unnecessary fear, sudden shock.

2. **Alibosh.** A glaringly obvious falsehood or exaggeration.

3. **Bimp.** A disappointment, a futile rage, a jilt.

4. **Bleesh.** An unpleasant picture; vulgar or obscene.

5. **Blurb.** Praise from one's self, inspired laudation.

6. **Bripkin.** One who half does things; second-hand, imitation.

7. **Cowcat.** An unimportant guest, an insignificant personality.

8. **Critch.** To array one's self in uncomfortable splendor.

9. **Culp.** A fond delusion, an imaginary attribute.

10. **Diabob.** An object of amateur art, adorned without taste.

11. **Digmix.** An unpleasant, uncomfortable or dirty occupation.

12. **Drillig.** A tiresome lingerer, one who talks too long.

13. **Edicle.** One who is educated beyond his intellect, a pedant.

14. **Eegot.** A selfishly interested friend, a lover of success.

15. **Elp.**   A tricky, sly or elusive person, a promiser.

16. **Fidgeltick.**   Food that it is a bore to eat; a taciturn person.

17. **Flooijab.**   An apparent compliment with a concealed sting.

18. **Frime.**   An educated heart, one who does the right thing.

19. **Fud.**   A state of disorder or déshabille, a mess.

20. **Frowk.**   A spicy topic, a half-wrong act, a sly suggestion.

21. **Geefoojet.**   An unnecessary thing, an article seldom used.

22. **Gixlet.**   One who has more heart than brains, an entertainer.

23. **Gloogo.**   Foolishly faithful without reward; loyal, fond.

24. **Goig.**   One whom one distrusts intuitively, suspicious.

25. **Gollohix.**   An untimely noise, a disturbance, especially at night.

26. **Golobrify.**   To adorn with unmeaning and extravagant ornament.

27. **Gorgule.**   A splendiferous, over-ornate object or gift.

28. **Gorm.**   A human hog; to take more than one's share.

29. **Gowyop.**   A perplexity wherein familiar things seem strange.

30. **Gubble.**   Society talk, the hum of foolish conversation.

31. **Huzzlecoo.**   An intimate talk, a confidential colloquy.

32. **Hygog.**   An unsatisfied desire, something out of one's reach.

33. **Hyprijimp.**   A man who does woman's work; one alone amid women.

34. **Igmoil.**   A sordid quarrel over money matters.

35. **Impkin.**   A superhuman pet, a baby in beast form.

36. **Iobink.**   An unplaceable resemblance, an inaccessible memory.

37. **Jip.**   A *faux pas*, a dangerous subject of conversation.

38. **Jirriwig.**   A traveller who does not see the country.

39. **Jujasm.**   An expansion of sudden joy after suspense.

40. **Jullix.**   A mental affinity, one with similar tastes or memory.

41. **Jurp.**   An impudent servant or underling, a saucy clerk.

42. **Kidloid.**   A precocious or self-assertive child. *Enfant terrible.*

43. **Kipe.**   To inspect appraisingly, as women do one another.

44. **Kripsle.**   An annoying physical sensation or defect.

45. **Lallify.**   To prolong a story tiresomely, or repeat a joke.

46. **Leolump.**   An interrupter of conversations, an egoistic bore.

47. **Looblum.**   Palatable but indigestible food; flattery.

48. **Machizzle.**   To attempt unsuccessfully to please, to try to like.

49. **Meem.**   An artificial half-light that women love; gloom.

50. **Mooble.**   A mildly amusing affair, a semi-interesting person.

51. **Moosoo.**   Sulky, out of sorts or out of order; delayed.

52. **Nink.** An " antique " resurrected for decorative effect.

53. **Nodge.** The only one of its kind, or having no mate.

54. **Nulkin.** The secret explanation, the inside history.

55. **Oofle.** A person whose name one cannot remember; to forget.

56. **Orobaldity.** Modern mysticism, a short cut to success.

57. **Ovotch.** A thing in style, the current fad.

58. **Paloodle.** To give unnecessary advice; one who thus bores.

59. **Pawdle.** One vicariously famous, or with undeserved prominence.

60. **Persotude.** Social warmth or magnetism, amount of popular favor.

61. **Pooje.** To embarrass; a regrettable discovery.

62. **Quink.** An expression or mood of anxious expectancy.

63. **Quisty.** Useful and reliable without being ornamental.

64. **Quoob.** A person or thing obviously out of place, a misfit.

65. **Rawp.** A reliably unreliable person, one always late.

66. **Rizgidget.** An inability to make up one's mind, an indecision.

67. **Rowtch.** To eat in extraordinary fashion, to gormandize.

68. **Skinje.** To feel shudderingly, to shrink from instinctively.

69. **Skyscrimble.** To go off at a tangent, mentally; to escape logic.

SLU   BURGESS ABRIDGED   VOR

70. **Slub.**	A mild indisposition which does not incapacitate.
71. **Snosh.**	Vain talk; a project that is born dead.
72. **Spigg.**	A decoration of overt vanity; to attract notice, paint.
73. **Spillix.**	Accidental good luck, uncharacteristically skilful.
74. **Splooch.**	One who doesn't know his own business; a failure.
75. **Spuzz.**	Mental force, aggressive intellectuality, stamina.
76. **Squinch.**	To watch and wait anxiously, hoping for a lucky turn.
77. **Tashivation.**	The art of answering without listening to questions.
78. **Thusk.**	Something that has quickly passed from one's life.
79. **Tintiddle.**	An imaginary conversation; wit coming too late.
80. **Udney.**	A beloved bore; one who loves but does not understand.
81. **Uglet.**	An unpleasant duty too long postponed.
82. **Unk.**	An unwelcome, inappropriate or duplicate present.
83. **Varm.**	The quintessence of sex; sex hatred or antipathy.
84. **Vilp.**	An unsportsmanlike player, a bad loser, a braggart.
85. **Voip.**	Food that gives no pleasure to the palate.
86. **Vorge.**	Voluntary suffering, unnecessary effort or exercise.
87. **Voriander.**	A woman who pursues men or demands attentions.

88. **Whinkle.** Hypocritical graciousness; to glow with vanity.

89. **Wijjicle.** A perverse household article, always out of order.

90. **Wog.** Food on the face; unconscious adornment of the person.

91. **Wowze.** A female fool, an unconsciously ridiculous woman.

92. **Wox.** A state of placid, satisfied contentment.

93. **Wumgush.** Women's insincere flattery of each other.

94. **Xenogore.** An interloper who keeps one from interesting things.

95. **Yab.** A monomaniac or fanatic, enthusiasm over one thing.

96. **Yamnoy.** A bulky, unmanageable object to be carried.

97. **Yod.** A ban or restriction on pleasant things.

98. **Yowf.** One whose importance exceeds his merit; a rich fool.

99. **Zeech.** A monologuist; one who is lively, but exhausting.

100. **Zobzib.** An amiable blunderer, one displaying misguided zeal.

BURGESS UNABRIDGED

A NEW DICTIONARY

Ag'o-wilt, *n.* 1. Sickening terror, sudden, unnecessary fear. 2. The passage of the heart past the epiglottis, going up. 3. Emotional insanity.

Ag'o-wilt, *v.* To almost-faint.

"What's that smell? Is it smoke? — Is it?" You throw open the door and have an agowilt; the staircase is in flames. But this is the fierce and wild variety. Agowilts tamed for domestic use, are far more common. The minute after you throw the burnt match into the waste-paper basket, the agowilt comes.

It may be but a single extra step which isn't there and the agowilt playfully paralyzes your heart. So a sudden jerk of the elevator, the startling stopping of the train, the automobile skidding, the roller-coaster looping the loop — bring agowilts.

Vicariously you suffer as well, when the trapeze performers swing in dizzying circles or do the "death dive."

"Good heavens! I left my bag in the train!" — an agowilt quite as painful. (See *Nulkin.*)

Why does your friend, reckless Robert, pause on the edge of the cliff? Merely to delight you with an agowilt.

When I taught Fanny, the flirt, to swim, and she found herself in water over her head, why did she scream and throw her arms about my neck? Was it truly an agowilt? (See *Varm.*)

> *'Twas not when Johnnie got the gun*
> *And pointed it at Jean;*
> *Nor when he played, in childish fun*
> *With father's razor keen —*
>
> *She did not agowilt until*
> *Her little brother said:*
> *"I just saw sister kissing Bill!"*
> *She agowilted dead.*

Al'i-bosh, *n.*   A glaringly obvious falsehood;
   something not meant to be actually believed;
   a picturesque overstatement.

A circus poster is an alibosh; so is a seed catalogue, a
woman's age and an actress's salary.   (See *Blurb.*)

There are verbal aliboshes too numerous to mention: " I
have had such a charming time!" and "No, I don't think
you're a bit too fat, you are just nice and plump."   (See *Gubble and Wumgush.*)

The saleswoman makes her living on the alibosh: "Yes, I
think that hat is very becoming."   She doesn't believe it, you
don't believe it — it's only a part of the game — like the lies
of horse-trading, the inspired notices of theatrical failures or
a prospectus of a gold mine.

> *The dentist, when he filled my tooth,*
> *   Filled me with alibosh;*
> *He said it wouldn't hurt, forsooth!*
> *   I knew he lied, b'gosh!*
>
> *But when he had one filled himself*
> *   They took an ounce or two*
> *Of chloroform from off the shelf.*
> *   No alibosh would do!*

Bimp, *n.* A disappointment, a futile rage.
Bimp, *v.* To cut, neglect, or forsake.
Bimped, *p.p.* Jilted, left.

As Mrs. Ezra P. McCormick stood in the middle of Myrtle Avenue at the corner of Grandview Street the trolley car came hurtling past, ten minutes behind time. Wildly she waved her parasol, but the car would not, did not stop! Mrs. McCormick got bimped. Her bimp was the more horrible, because the conductor turned and grinned at her, and three men on the rear platform laughed, for Mrs. McCormick was very fat. (See *Jurp.*)

Did you get that raise in your salary on New Year's day, or did you get bimped? Were you forgotten on Christmas? Did you draw to a flush and fail to fill? You got bimped. Did you find you had no cash in your pocket when it came time to pay the waiter? Did that firm cancel its order? Bimps.

What did Mrs. Harris's servant girl do on the very afternoon of the dinner party? She bimped Mrs. Harris! She packed her imitation-leather suitcase, grabbed her green umbrella and walked away.

The girl who stood "Waiting at the church" got the biggest bimp of all. (See *Agowilt.*)

Bimp not, that ye be not bimped! (See *Machizzle.*)

> *I got a bimp, the other night,*
>   *It bimped me good and hard;*
> *I drew to fill a flush, and got*
>   *A different colored card.*
>
> *But still, I bluffed it out and won;*
>   *A well-filled pot I crimped —*
> *And three good hands of treys and pairs,*
>   *And one full house, got bimped!*

Bleesh, *n.* 1. An unpleasant picture; vulgar or obscene art. 2. An offensive comic-supplement form of humor.

Bleesh, *a.* Revolting, disgusting, coarse.

Comic valentines are very bleesh; the newspaper " comic strip " with the impossible adventure ending in catastrophic brutality; stars, exclamation points and "Wows!" Especially a bull-dog, biting the seat of a man's trousers and revolving like a pinwheel — this is a bleesh. (See *Frowk.*)

Crayon enlargements of photographs of your uncle in his Odd Fellows' uniform are bleesh — Kodak snap-shots and flashlights of banquet groups.

Your practical-joking friend sends you bleesh foreign postcards from abroad; and your chauffeur revels in bleesh pictures of crime, with an X showing " where the body was found."

To the Philistine of the Middle West, the nude in art is bleesh. To the eye-glassed school-ma'am of Brooklyn, the paintings of Cubists and Futurists are bleesher still. (See *Ovotch.*)

> *I gazed upon a bleesh, and saw*
> *'Twas stupid, crude and coarse;*
> *Its wit was dull, its art was raw,*
> *It had nor wit nor force.*
>
> *And then my niece, a virgin pure,*
> *But used to clever folk,*
> *Laughed at that bleesh till I was sure*
> *I'd somehow missed the joke.*

Blurb, *n.*   1. A flamboyant advertisement; an inspired testimonial.   2. Fulsome praise; a sound like a publisher.

Blurb, *v.*   1. To flatter from interested motives; to compliment oneself.

On the " jacket " of the " latest " fiction, we find the blurb; abounding in agile adjectives and adverbs, attesting that this book is the " sensation of the year; " the blurb tells of " thrills " and " heart-throbs," of " vital importance " and " soul satisfying revelation." The blurb speaks of the novel's " grip " and " excitement." (See *Alibosh.*)

The circus advertiser started the blurb, but the book publisher discovered a more poignant charm than alliterative polysyllables. " It holds you from the first page —"

Now, you take this " Burgess Unabridged "— it's got a jump and a go to it — it's got a hang and a dash and a swing to it that pulls you right out of the chair, dazzles your eyes, and sets your hair to curling. It's an epoch-making, heart-tickling, gorglorious tome of joy!

So, were not my publishers old-fashioned, would this my book be blurbed.

> If " Burgess Unabridged," I say,
>   " Fulfils a long-felt want,"
> Don't mind my praise, nor yet the way
>   In which I voice my vaunt.
>
> Don't let my adjectives astute
>   Your peace of mind disturb;
> It's " bold," it's " clever " and it's " cute,"
>   And so is this my blurb!

Brip′kin, *n.* 1. One who half does things; not a thoroughbred. 2. A suburbanite, commuter.

Brip′kin, *a.* Off color; second-rate; shabby-genteel, a little out of style.

The bripkin invites a girl to the theatre, but he takes her in a street-car — on a rainy night, too! The bripkin tips the waiter less than ten per cent. of his bill. He carries a cane, but does not wear gloves. He frequents the manicure, and wears near-silk shirts, with frayed cuffs. His hat is " the latest " but his coat sleeves are shiny.

The female bripkin has a button off her shoe; she wears white gloves, but they are badly soiled. She wears a three-quarter-length grey squirrel coat.

American champagne is bripkin — Key-West cigars and domestic beer, and imitation coffee. (See *Voip.*)

A bripkin umbrella is made of gloria.

The second-rate suburb of a great city is a bripkin, and so is he who dwells therein. He wears a watch-chain strung across his vest. (See *Mooble.*)

Bripkins are the marked-down gowns and suits, at the tail end of the season; and the green hat, " reduced from $18.75."

> *A Bripkin sat in a trolley car,*
> *And his eyes were bright and tiny;*
> *His collars and cuffs were slightly soiled,*
> *But his finger nails were shiny.*
>
> *A girl came in with run-over heels,*
> *And the Bripkin up and kissed her!*
> *But I knew, by her mangy ermine muff,*
> *That she was his Bripkin sister.*

BRIPKIN

Cow'cat, *n.* 1. A person whose main function is to occupy space. An insignificant, or negligible personality. 2. A guest who contributes nothing to the success of an affair; one invited to fill up, or from a sense of duty. 3. An innocent bystander.

The cowcat will not talk, but oh, how he listens! How he watches! How he criticises! But why speak of the cowcat as " he "? They usually have large, black satin, placid abdomens, or else they are thin and nervous, with acid eyes. (See *Yowf.*)

How describe a cowcat? There's nothing about it to describe. It's a jelly-fish — a heavy jelly-fish, however. It sits upon your stomach, like a nightmare.

Cowcats fill hotel chairs, and the rockers of summer verandahs, knitting gossip. (See *Mooble.*)

Your wife's relatives?

> *The cowcats in the corners sat,*
> *And brooded 'gainst the wall,*
> *And some were thin and some were fat,*
> *But none would talk at all.*
>
> *The atmosphere grew thick and cold —*
> *It had begun to jell,*
> *When I, with desperation bold,*
> *Arose, and gave a yell!*

Critch, *v.* 1. To array oneself in uncomfortable splendor.

Critch'et-y, *a.* 1. Conspicuous and stiff; garbed elaborately, especially on a hot day. 2. Painfully aware of one's costume.

Oh, that stiff collar! That binding corset! Those burning feet in the tight shoes! Yes, you are critched, but at the same time you have the moral support of being becomingly and fashionably clad. A critch is half pride and half madness — it's the martyrdom of fashion. (See *Vorge.*)

The unaccustomed exquisite in his hard boiled shirt, stiff cuffs and high collar stands critchety, but willing to endure the agonies of the aristocracy.

You may be too cool in decolleté, or too warm in your furs, but vanity vanquishes the critch.

You are critched when you have a picture taken, but that radiant smile survives. At private theatricals all the actors are critched with tights and swords and furbelows — trying to appear at ease. (See *Wowze.*)

The banker is critched with his silk hat in a high wind; and the dowager, as she carefully arranges her skirts when she is seated. But to be properly critched, you must be a Japanese countess, putting on stays for the first time in your artless, lavender life.

> *A sovereign's lot is sad and strange,*
> *For kings and queens, they say,*
> *Are all uneasy; they must change*
> *Their clothes ten times a day!*

> *Ah, robes and uniforms and crowns*
> *Are glorious things, I know,*
> *And queens do wear expensive gowns —*
> *They must be critchety, though!*

Culp, *n.* 1. A fond delusion; an imaginary attribute. 2. What one would like to be, or
thinks oneself.
Cul′pid, *a.* 1. Visionary, non-existent. 2. Not
proved; autohypnotized.

Many women have the culp that they are beautiful, men
that they are irresistible, shrewd, or interesting.

A culpid actor is one who thinks he can act, but can't. His
culp is that he is making a hit. (See *Splooch.*)

The mother has the baby culp; but the infant to other eyes
is not so wonderful.

The woman with the culpid taste thinks that no other
woman knows how to dress. (See *Wumgush.*)

The author who has had three letters requesting his auto-
graph, has the culp that he is popular.

That young man who stays till 11.45 P. M. has a culp that
he has fascinated yawning Ysobel.

She had a culp that she was fair,
In fact, that she was pretty;
Alas, she bought her beauty where
They sold it, in the city.

And now her culp is: Looks will lie;
And her delight is huge —
She thinks that none suspects the dye,
The powder and the rouge!

Di′a-bob, *n.*   1. An object of amateur art; anything improbably decorated; hand-painted.
2. Any decoration or article of furniture
manufactured between 1870 and 1890.
Di-a-bob′i-cal, *a.*   Ugly, while pretending to
be beautiful.

Who invented the diabob?   The infamy is attributed to
John Ruskin.   At any rate, humble things began to lose the
dignity of the commonplace; the rolling-pin became exotic in
the parlor.   The embroidery blossomed in hectic tidies,
splashes and drapes.   Hand-painting was discovered.
So, from the Spencerian skylark to the perforated "God
Bless Our Home."   Now the jigsaw was master; now, the
incandescent point that tortured wood and leather into nightmare designs.   Plaques began their vogue. (See *Gefoojet*.)
Diabobical was the hammered brasswork; diabobical the
sofa cushion limned with Gibson heads.   The decorative fan,
genteel; the pampas grass, dyed bright purple; the macramé
bags and the seaweed pictures passed; came the embossed
pictures stuck on bean-pots and molasses jugs; came the
esthetic cat-tail and piano-lamp, "A Yard of Daisies," and
burnt match receivers and catch-alls, ornamented by the family genius.
Ah,   Where are the moustache cups of yesteryear?

This object made of celluloid,
This thing so wildly plushed,—
How grossly Art has been annoyed!
How Common Sense has blushed!

And yet, these diabobs, perhaps
Are scarcely more outré
Than pictures made by Cubist chaps,
Or Futurists, today!

14

DIABOB

See also GEFOOJET, GOLOBRIFY *and* GORGULE

Dig′mix, *n.* 1. An unpleasant, uncomfortable, or dirty occupation. 2. A disagreeable or unwelcome duty.

Dig′mix, *v.* To engage in a necessary but painful task.

The type of the digmix is cleaning fish. At first it is disgusting, untidy, uncomfortable. Then, you begin to enjoy it, rather; and finally, as the clean, finished product of your skill appears, there is the refreshing sense of duty well done. (See *Gloogo.*)

So with all household digmixes, stuffing feathers into pillows, peeling onions, taking up carpets, putting up stove pipes, beating rugs, attending to the furnace and washing dishes. You loathe the work, but, when it is finished, you're so glad you did it.

The mental digmix is less satisfactory, but just as necessary. Discharging the cook is a digmix. Breaking the news of a death, refusing a man who has proposed, explaining just why you came home at 2 A. M., accompanying a child to a dentist's, getting a divorce, waiting on a querulous invalid, having a lawsuit with a neighbor,— all are digmixes. (See *Moosoo.*)

Why, to some, the mere eating of an orange or a grape fruit is a digmix! They feel as if they ought to take a bath and then go straight to bed.

But why enlarge upon a painful subject? After all, life is just one digmix after another.

> *Poor Jones was in a digmix — he*
> *Had blown his right front tire;*
> *He worked from half past one till three;*
> *Oh, how he did perspire!*
>
> *But that was not what crazed his mind;*
> *A digmix worse than that*
> *Confronted him — he had to find*
> *That day a good, cheap flat!*

Dril′lig, *n.*   A tiresome lingerer; a button-holer.
Dril′li-ga-tor, *n.*   Same as drillig.
Dril′li-gate, *v.*   1. To detain a person when he
wants to go to work or get away.   2. To talk
unceasingly at an inconvenient time.

He rings you up on the telephone, or she rings you up, and
drilligates you by the hour, if you are too kind-hearted to hang
up the receiver.   Of course she has nothing important to say;
you know she is leaning back in her chair, smiling, and eating
chocolates.   (See *Lallify.*)

The drillig calls in the rush hours of business, sits down,
crosses his legs, and nothing moves except his mouth.   He is
never busy and never hurried.   He catches you on the street
corner, holds you by the button or lapel, in the middle of a
cursing stream of pedestrians, and tells you a long, dull story.
" Just a minute, now, I just want to tell you about —"   The
Ancient Mariner was a drillig.   (See *Xenogore.*)

The public speaker at the banquet rises with a bland smile
and looks at his watch.   " The hour is so late," he says, " and
there are so many more interesting speakers to be heard from,
that I shall detain you with only a few words —" and he
drilligs on for an hour and six minutes by the clock.

The drillig catches you in a corner at the club and tells you
the story of his play; the young mother nails you to the sofa
with her smile, and drilligs you about Baby.

The book agent, anchored in the front door at meal times, is
the master drilligator of them all.   (See *Persotude.*)

> *I was rushing for the station,*
> *Had to catch the 5.11,*
> *When he caught me, seized a button,*
> *And began to talk — Oh, Heaven!*
>
> *For the Drillig was a golfer,*
> *And I knew he'd talk his fill;*
> *So I cut that button off my coat —*
> *He is talking to it still!*

18

Ed'i-cle, *n.* 1. One who is educated beyond his intellect; a pedant. 2. One who is proficient in theory, but poor in practice.

In old times, they spoke of " Book learning " and worshiped the edicled fool. But we are wiser today and know the hollowness of the edicle.

The edicle is the college professor who has listened to his own talk so long that he has mistaken knowledge for wisdom. The book-worm who has learned to believe that literature is greater than life. (See *Snosh.*)

A woman is an edicle, who prates " new thought " and juggles the trite phrases of a philosophy too heavy for her comprehension. (See *Orobaldity.*) A man is an edicle when he quotes Browning or Karl Marx or Herbert Spencer. Most clergymen are edicles, and persons who rave over pictures they don't understand.

The book reviewer who can't write a book himself, is an edicle. The dramatic critic is an edicle, for he has failed as a playwright. (See *Yowf.*)

The college girl who can't cook is an edicle; the young medico, newly graduated, with an " M.D." painted on him still fresh, and wet and green,— a mere mass of quivering Latin words. All editors are edicles.

> *Josephus is an edicle,*
> *A Doctor wise is he;*
> *Oh, no! — not doctor medical —*
> *Only a Ph. D.*
>
> *His brain is like a phonograph's,*
> *And he would starve, unless*
> *He'd started writing monographs*
> *On " How to BE Success."*

Ee'got, *n.*   1. A fair-weather friend; one who is over-friendly with a winner. A success-worshiper.

Ee'goid, *a.*   1. Self-interested, mercenary.

The eegot slaps the favorite sprinter on the back and cheers him on, but switches interest when he fails to finish. The eegot takes the popular side of every subject, curries favor with the rich and prosperous, and is attentive to the belle of the ball.

Four feet away from the popular hero, and you will find the eegots clustered close. (See *Elp.*)

The eegot votes for the one whom he thinks will win — he believes that the rich can do no wrong.

The eegot always wears " the latest," and reads only " the best sellers." (See *Ovotch.*)

He suddenly discovers his poor country cousin,— after she has married the Lieutenant-Governor.

Molasses draws flies — prosperity breeds the egoid parasite.

> *When you are rich and great and grand,*
> *The eegot needs you badly;*
> *He wags his tail, he licks your hand,*
> *He lets you kick him gladly.*

> *But when your fortune's gone, and fame,*
> *Where is the eegot then?*
> *Oh, he is capering just the same —*
> *But now for other men!*

Elp, *n.* 1. A tricky, sly or subtle person; one who evades his responsibilities. 2. An ingenious ruse; sharp practice.

El′pine, *a.* Disappointing; plausibly apologetic.

The elp is a clever promiser, who doesn't make good. You never can pin him down,— he always escapes you. He won't do what he has promised, or pay his debts; but his explanations are always all-but-convincing.

The tradesman is an elp, who promises to deliver those provisions in time for dinner, and always has a good excuse. The ladies' tailor is an elp — the suit is never done on time. (See *Goig.*)

At the employment agency, the elps abound. They are always " sure to come " on Thursday. Friday and Saturday pass by.

The elp never quite knows, but would never confess his ignorance. It is impossible to get him to say either " Yes " or " No."

Most infamous among the elps is the philandering suitor, who is attentive to you for years and years, keeping serious men away, and yet who will not propose. (See *Xenogore.*)

> *He promised he would pay in June —*
> *Then August — then September;*
> *And then he sang the same old tune:*
> *He promised for December.*

> *His sister died — his wife fell ill —*
> *His brother needed help;*
> *And I believed his tales, until*
> *I saw he was an elp.*

Fid'gel-tick, *n.*   Food that it is a bore to eat;
anything requiring painstaking and ill-re-
quited effort.   2. A taciturn person, one from
whom it is hard to get information.

The fidgeltick tastes good, but is it really worth while?
Come now,— doesn't salad really bore you — unless it is
served, as in California, at the beginning of a meal, while
you are still hungry?   Broiled live lobster!   How succulent,
yet how meagre its reward to the appetite!   Frogs' legs are
fidgelticks, and shad and grape fruit and pistachios.   Why
can't such tasteful delicacies be built with the satisfactory
architecture of the banana?   The artichoke gives perhaps the
minimum of reward with the maximum of effect.   (See *Voip.*)
And who does not flinch at a Bent's water cracker?
To make cranberry sauce with the skins in, and cherry
pie with the stones, should be against the law.
So it is, to extract information from a railroad official after
an accident.   Interviewing the master of a steamer is like
getting the meat out of a butternut, or the flesh out of a
shrimp.   Sooner or later, you will give him up in discouragement.   He's a fidgeltick!   (See *Jurp.*)
Politely you inquire of a ticket seller at the theatre; you
might as well talk with a foreigner, or a deaf man.   All, all
are fidgelticks!

> *I wish that I could eat as fast*
> *   As actors, on the stage;*
> *Five minutes does a dinner last —*
> *   No fidgelticks enrage.*

> *If they should dine on soft boiled eggs*
> *   In some new problem play,*
> *Or lobsters broiled, or frogs' hind legs —*
> *   What would the actors say?*

Floo′i-jab, *n.* 1. A cutting remark, disguised in sweetness. 2. A ladylike trouble-maker.
Floo′i-jab, *v.* To make a sarcastic comment in a feminine manner.
Floo-i-jab′ber-y, *n.* Feline amenity.

For the flooijab of commerce, see the typical Ethel-Clara dialogues in the comic papers; and yet, one cannot describe the tone — the sugared smile that gives the shot its sting. (See *Varm.*)

Anent women's looks, the flooijabs fly fastest.

" Oh, yes, Helen *used* to be a very beautiful girl! "

" We're not so young as we used to be, but you do look awfully pretty, *today*."

" No,— I don't think you look a day older,— except when you are tired."

" I'm *so* delighted that you are engaged to Harry! How did you do it —' holding the thought '? "

" They do say she's awfully fast — but I never noticed anything — I think she's sweet. Too bad she's talked about so! "

" I think you gave an awfully good performance — of course, you weren't a Bernhardt, but then . . ." (See *Wumgush.*)

" I'm so sorry you didn't make good; it's a shame! I think you did awfully well, really! "

" I thought your little story was so good. I suppose influence with the editors counts a lot,— doesn't it? "

You think they talk of men and mice,
   Of operas, and cabs;
Ah no! Beneath those phrases nice,
   They're shooting flooijabs.

No man can know — but women may
   Interpret women's smiles —
It's what they mean — not what they say,
   That stings in women's wiles.

Frime, *n.*   1. An educated heart.   2. One who
always does the right thing at the right time;
a person who can be depended upon in time
of need.

The mind is cultivated until it is hypercivilized, but where
is the educated heart?   The frime, like the fool, is born, not
made; no one has told him when to speak and when to remain
silent, or when to laugh and when to cry.   (See *Zobzib.*)

The frime knows when you are hungry, when you are
thirsty and when you would be let alone.   He speaks a person's name so clearly when he introduces you that you can
actually understand.

The frime knows when to come and when to go; he makes
the lion as comfortable as the humblest guest.   He sends you
fruit instead of flowers.   The frime knows the etiquette of
life and love and death; he likes you in spite of your faults.
As a lover, he never makes you or himself ridiculous.   As a
consoler, he is never guilty of that most ironic bromide: "If
there is anything I can do, let me know."   (See *Spuzz.*)

> *When I was down and out, one time —*
> *Believe me, 'twasn't funny! —*
> *I chanced upon a thorough frime;*
> *Unasked, he lent me money.*
>
> *When I was rich, and he was poor*
> *I lent to help his need;*
> *And did he pay it back?   Why, sure!*
> *There was a frime, indeed!*

Fud, *n.*   1. In a state of déshabille, or confusion.   2. A mess, or half-done job.
Fud'dy, *a.*   Disordered, untidy, unkempt.

What is a fud?   A woman in curl papers and her oldest kimona.   A man in his shirt-sleeves with his suspenders hanging from two buttons, down behind.   It is a half built house; half cooked potatoes on the back of the stove.   Anyone in stocking feet.   (See *Frowk.*)

No one can help being fuddy, at times, so long as there is house-cleaning and moving to be done; but some fuds are fuddier than others.   A house that is being reshingled, for instance, is far less fuddy than an actress washing greasepaint off her face, or stumbling in a peignoir through a Pullman car, her hair tousled, to reach the dressing-room.   (See *Spigg.*)

Ellen's top bureau drawer is fuddy, after she has tried to find "that veil."   The parlor and library are fuddy after the reception.

It's an unpleasant subject.   Let us end it, with the mention of half-dried wash and unwashed dishes in the kitchen sink.   (See *Uglet.*)

> *I call you fuddy — how severe*
> *My accents disapproving!*
> *And yet, you cannot help it, dear,*
> *Alas, for we are moving!*
>
> *The house is fuddy — so am I,*
> *And so is everybody!*
> *The moving van is late, so why*
> *Should we not all be fuddy?*

Frowk, *n.*   1. A spicy topic.   2. An action considered to be about half wrong.

Frow'cous, *a.*   Nice, but naughty, or considered so; piquantly provocative; risqué, pertaining to sex.

How frowcous is the limerick, in its most perfect form! That frowk which it is just barely possible to recite at a dinner party:— " There was a young lady so thin, that she slightly resembled a pin; don't think that I'd creep to her window and peep — I was told by a friend, who looked in."

'Tis a frowcous epoch — eugenics, white slavery, and the " dangerous age " are now the vogue, and a play that's not a frowk can scarcely make a hit on Broadway.   (See *Ovotch*.)

In the era of " sensibility "— when ladies had the vapors, the sight of a man shaving himself was frowcous.   Now, we subscribe for the foreign illustrated comic papers, and speak boldly concerning " Damaged Goods."   (See *Bleesh*.)

Once a turkey trot was frowcous; bare feet and cocktails — but little is frowcous now.   There are *so* many " things that a young girl ought to know! "

> *A frowcous tale one day I told*
> *To Revered Eli Meek.*
> *His laughter he could scarcely hold —*
> *It lasted for a week.*
>
> *He couldn't stop his wild guffaws;*
> *To calm his merry gale*
> *He had to leave the church, because*
> *He had to tell the tale!*

Ge-fooj'et, *n.* 1. An unnecessary thing; an article seldom used. 2. A tool; something one ought to throw away, and doesn't. 3. The god of unnecessary things.

Ge-fooj'et-y, *a.* 1. Superfluous. 2. Pertaining to an old garret.

" Oh, no, I don't want to throw that away yet; I'll give it away to somebody, some time," or " We may need it."   This is the doctrine of Gefoojet, which, preached and practiced in New England, has outlived the dogma of infant damnation. A thousand housewife martyrs have suffered years of persecution, testifying to the sublime nonsense. (See *Quisty.*)

In my grandmother's wood-house closet, were ten thousand pieces of folded brown paper, and one hundred miles of string, salvaged from by-gone packages in sacrifice to Gefoojet.

Old letters, half used scrap-books, bottles, boxes and fragments of hardware accumulate unceasingly.

What is a Gefoojet?   It's something you haven't used for two years, an old magazine or your wedding dress.

This is what cupboards and closets, top shelves, whatnots and garrets were invented for.—Gefoojets.

Have you a camera?   Go forth and garner gefoojets.

" That thing " you keep because it was given by a dear friend — beware of it —'tis a gefoojet.   (See *Thusk.*)

> *Seven years I kept her letters — how*
> *Some time, I hoped to read them!*
> *Alas, they are gefoojets, now!*
> *I know I'll never need them.*
>
> *But still gefoojetry survives,*
> *And makes us slaves to Things;*
> *Each day Gefoojet, all our lives,*
> *Some useless present brings!*

Gix'let, *n.* 1. One who has more heart than brains. 2. An inveterate host; an irresistible entertainer.

Gix'let-y, *a.* Brutal kindness; misguided hospitality; an overdose of welcome.

" Have some more of this — please do — I *insist* — I made it myself! " So says the gixlet, as she passes the piccalilli. (See *Vorge.*)

The gixlet insists upon paying your fare everywhere, he begs your pardon, when you step on his foot. He introduces you to everybody he meets. In public, he praises you with excruciating conspicuousness. At home, he insists upon your going to church, or showing you over his new house.

He says, "Why haven't you been before?" (See *Wumgush.*)

He takes you on long walks when you visit him in the country, and want just to sit on the verandah and loaf.

The gixlet in the club orders drinks when you don't want them, and insists upon your drinking them, because he does. The gixlet, in short, is the joyous, friendly dog, that leaps with muddy paws upon your clean, white trousers.

> *The Gixlets entertained me till*
> *I thought I'd die the death;*
> *His wife and he could not keep still,*
> *Though I was out of breath.*

> *They showed me things, they made me gorge,*
> *Then walked me round the farm;*
> *That night, I killed them both, by George!*
> *Tell me, where was the harm?*

Gloo'go, *n.* 1. A devoted adherent of a person, place or thing. 2. A married person in love with his or her spouse after the first year. 3. Anything that can be depended upon.

Gloo'go, *a.* Loyal, constant. Foolishly faithful without pay.

Do you take cold baths all through January, February and March? You're a gloogo,— especially if you don't talk about it. (See *Yab.*)

Do you work over hours at the office? Do you come downtown early? Do you run in on Sundays and finish up a little batch of business? You're a gloogo.

The gloogo, when young, studies his home lessons, instead of going to that Saturday night dance. In after-life he attends church every Sunday, and puts a quarter in the plate. If he plays golf, he prefers a rainy, cold day. (See *Vorge.*)

The gloogo elevator runs all night — but it's a curiosity.

The family gloogo comes to dinner regularly on Wednesdays and Sundays. (See *Xenogore.*) Elsie Peach's gloogo calls every day and always invites her to everything. Mrs. Valentine's maid-servant is a gloogo — she loves to have extra company for dinner.

You are a gloogo, if you read Burgess Unabridged all through.

> *John Smith was a gloogo of forty-five,*
>   *And he worked like a piece of machinery;*
> *He was fond of his wife (who was still alive),*
>   *And he always took lunch in a beanery.*

> *He went to church, and he didn't drink,*
>   *And he had no sins, no mystery;*
> *And that'll be all about him, I think,—*
>   *For Gloogos seldom make history.*

Goig, *n.* A suspected person; one whom we distrust instinctively; an unfounded bias; an inexplainable aversion.

Goig'some, *a.* Dubious; requiring references or corroboration.

To one from Missouri, the world is full of goigs. Well you have to "show me," too, when the new janitor takes possession of the cellar — he's a goig. There's the man with the perpetual smile; he's a goig. Why do we watch the gentleman whose collar buttons behind, or the dog who doesn't wag his tail? There's something goigsome about them. He "listens well,"— *but!* I ha'e me doots! (See *Eegot.*)

To the fondly doting mother, her son's sweetheart is always a goig. When he's engaged, she is still more goigsome. Once married, and the suspense is over. (See *Frime.*)

Would you be a goig? Then shave your upper lip and grow a chin beard.

The servile affability of an English shopkeeper, rubbing his hands — how goigsome! So is your wife's man-friend, and the new cook.

But, best of all goigs — or worst — the man who says: "Oh, I'll surely pay it back next week, at latest!" (See *Elp.*)

> *The dividends are ten percent,*
> *The stock " is going to rise,"*
> *" It's going to make the fortune of*
> *Each lucky man that buys."*

> *But still, I think I'll not invest,*
> *I do not know just why,—*
> *But with a Goig, it is best*
> *To let your neighbor try!*

Gol'lo-hix, *n.* 1. An untimely annoyance, especially when one wishes to sleep. 2. An auditory nuisance.

Of course, when you put up at the Fleetville Hotel Imperial, you got a room in the rear, looking out over the railroad station and the trains ran all night, backing and switching, raising a fine gollohix. But the side rooms were just as bad; there was a gollohix windmill creaking incessantly.

Further back in the country a dog will make the best gollohix, baying at the moon, or yelping at a woodchuck.

So let's come to the city. It's all night in the Pullman, and the gollohix they make with the milk-cans and switch-engines won't last but three or four hours.

Why try to describe the gollohix? It's the piano in the next flat at midnight; it's the turkey-trotting overhead; it's the phonograph across the hall. (See *Jujasm.*)

Why do they put in your neighbor's coal so late in the evening, when you have tonsilitis? The coal-man loves a gollohix, as a chauffeur loves a cut-out motor, as a city child loves firecrackers on the 3rd of July.

A musical comedy makes a good gollohix when you sit in the front row next to the drum, but a crying baby at four o'clock in the morning makes the best of all. (See *Kidloid.*)

Wait a minute — I forgot the man who practices the trombone or the cornet, just across the airshaft — that's a gollohix to dream about!

> *A New Year's Eve in gay New York,*
> *Fire engines at a fire,*
> *A parrot that doth squawk and squawk*
> *Are gollohixes dire.*

> *If gollohixes all could be*
> *Escaped, I'd thank my stars,*
> *But Gollohix the Great is he*
> *Who snores in sleeping-cars!*

Go-lob-ri-fac′tion, *n.* 1. An object which has suffered extravagant decoration. 2. A composition superspiced with adjectives.

Go-lob-ri-fac′tu-rer, *n.* A mad architect, or designer.

Go-lob′ri-fy, *v.* To adorn excessively; to add excruciating and unmeaning ornament.

Golobrifaction is the extravagant exaggeration of art. One may golobrify pastry, jellies, salads; or literature, with decadent phrases.

Golobrifaction is the art of supersweetening, or the flourish of eccentric adornment. (See *Diabob.*)

Topiary gardening golobrifies the country residence of the aristocrat; humbler abodes are golobrified with cast iron stags or plaster statues of nervous nymphs.

The lover golobrifies his *billets doux* with ardent adverbs. The ambitious builder golobrifies his villas with the fret-saw and the turning-lathe. (See *Gorgule.*)

Trading-stamp furniture, Spencerian flourishes, imitation castles, parsley decorations, notched turnips, oranges and radishes, cheap picture-frames, perfumery bottles, boars' heads, fishes with tails in their mouths, gingerbread men — all are golobrifactions.

The wedding cake of the millionaire is a golobriboblifaction. *Art nouveau* would require still another syllable. After all, is there much difference between a valentine and a formal Italian garden?

> *Her gown it was golobrified*
> *With flounces, tucks and shirrs,*
> *With laces trimmed, with ribbons tied,*
> *With buttons, fringe and furs.*

> *Like unnamed tropic bird her look,—*
> *For, putting Art in action,*
> *Her spouse, a famous pastry cook,*
> *Made that golobrifaction!*

Gor'gule, *n.* 1. An unwished-for gift; an unnecessary, splendiferous object. 2. Elaborate bad taste.

Gor'gu-lous, *a.* Ornamental, but not useful.

A gorgule is the imitation malachite clock, the fancy brass lamp, the green plush sofa, gorgulous with curves, writhing spirals, tassels, gimp and fringe. (See *Diabob.*)

A hand-embroidered necktie is a gorgule. So are lacy, frilled, beribboned boudoir-caps, without any boudoir; and fancy smoking jackets; and corset-covers with chiffon roses, theatrical act drops and scenic interiors,— anything too royal for humble use. (See *Golobrifaction.*)

Most wedding presents are gorgules. "Heavens, I wish someone would break that!" Need one describe the gorgule? A brass-and-onyx prodigy. A celluloid toilet set, in a plush casket, a chandelier of the epoch of 1880, a silver-plated ice-pitcher, or a set of lemonade-tumblers in colored glass. (See *Gefoojet.*)

Ever receive a loving-cup, grand and gorgulous? Once you were proud of it; now you're willing to have the children lug it to the seashore and shovel it full of sand. Why did you subscribe for that large folio *edition de luxe* "Masterpieces of Foreign Art," a gorgule in nine monstrous volumes — price $85.75?

Don't forget that eiderdown fan. It's a gorgule. Give it to the cook.

Behold this gorgulated chair —
A weird, upholsterrific blunder!
It doesn't wonder why it's there,
So don't encourage it to wonder;

For Gorgules such as this don't know
That they're impossible, and therefore
They go right on existing, so
This is the whyness of their wherefore.

Gorm, *n.*   A human hog; a practical egoist.
Gorm, *v.*   To take or desire more than one's
  proper share; to act greedily.
Gor'mid, *a.*   Selfish, individualistic.

The gorm, when you offer him a cigar, puts it in his pocket
and says he " will smoke it after dinner." When he loses his
watch, he offers a reward which shrinks amazingly when his
property is returned and he is sure of it back.   (See *Igmoil.*)
The gorm never pays for his round of drinks.   He manages so that the other fellow shall settle for the taxi and the
tickets.   He will never move up in the trolley-car or take his
bundle from the seat.   On the railway, he manages successfully to occupy four places at once.
The gorm is the woman who tries to get in ahead of the
line which forms at the ticket office.   She monopolizes the
most attractive man in the room to the exclusion of her sisters.   At the bargain counter the gorm holds three waists
while she examines a fourth.
Children gorm candy and ice-cream; men gorm free lunches,
and women in Pullman cars gorm the ladies' room for hours
and hours, behind locked doors.   (See *Spigg.*)
And all girls gorm love, or try to gorm it.

> *He gormed the fireplace, standing there*
>   *With coat tails to the flame*
> *With easy grace, without a care*
>   *For us who, shivering, came.*
>
> *He gormed the magazines, and sat*
>   *On papers by the dozen;*
> *But at our club we're used to that —*
>   *Our gormid English cousin!*

Gow'yop, *n.*   1. A state of perplexity, wherein familiar persons or things seem strange.   2. A person in an unfamiliar guise.

Have you ever been "turned around," coming out of a theatre, after an exciting play? Right is left and west is east. You are in a gowyop. It is long before you can turn yourself about and make the world seem normal.

The husband who has just shaved off his beard is a gowyop to his wife. And his wife is a gowyop, after she has tinted her hair bright red. (See *Spigg.*)

The gowyop is like that room you see in the mirror,— so like, and yet so different. Your house, the day after the funeral, is a gowyop — everything seems so strange.

A pretty child, with his two front teeth out; a person you haven't seen for many years and you now behold grown up; a son or a daughter who has just been married, are gowyops. So is the dignified old gentleman in the bathing suit. Or, that aristocratic dowager, who, when the house is on fire, appears in her night-gown; and your cook, when she is "dressed up."

To the bachelor of science, returning after four years at college, home is a gowyop, too. (See *Thusk.*)

> *All in a gowyop I descried*
> *An unfamiliar world;*
> *All upside down, I vainly tried*
> *To get myself uncurled.*
>
> *But I was inside out, till when*
> *I met my wife — the sight*
> *Quite turned me outside in again —*
> *She'd bleached her black hair white!*

Gub′ble, *n.* 1. A murmuring of many voices. 2. Society chatter.

Gub′ble, *v.* To indulge in meaningless conversation.

Gub′ble-go, *n.* 1. A crowded reception, a talking contest.

It's like some huge, slimy reptile, with a hundred mouths, all murmuring. As you are admitted to the house, as the servant takes your hat and cane, the far-off sounds of gubbling strike you with terror; but it must be done. In you go. Everyone is talking, but no one is listening. Say anything you like — it will be lost in the gubble.

There's gubble in a wordy play. There's gubble at the steamer when you see a friend off for Europe — a flattering gubble, after you have performed in public. (See *Wumqush.*)

Letters of condolence usually consist of gubble. Editorials about marine or railway disasters are gubble. So are funeral sermons. (See *Alibosh.*)

I entered, and I heard the hum
  Of multitudinous gubble;
And I was terrified and dumb,
  Anticipating trouble.

When I remarked that hens had lice,
  (Not knowing what I said),
My hostess smiled, and said " How nice!
  Let me present Miss Stead!"

HUZZLECOO

Huz′zle-coo, *n.*　1. An intimate talk; a " heart-to-heart " conversation; a private confidential chat.　2. A flirtation.

A huzzlecoo is an animated conversation between two women over the back fence.　It is a business talk between two partners and their credit-man behind the locked doors of the office; it is the directors' meeting which results in Jones being appointed.

Ward politicians hold huzzlecoos in the back rooms of saloons and make up their " slates."　Mother and daughter hold a huzzlecoo in Nellie's pink cretonne bedroom over " that young man " who has become so attentive.　After the baseball captain and his manager have a huzzlecoo, Five-Base Murphy is put into the box.

But if you've never heard two girls discussing a man, or sat in the front parlor with Moony Mamie, the Merry Man-eater, till 2 A. M.— then I pity you; you'll never know what a good hot huzzlecoo means.　(See *Voriander.*)

> *The huzzlecoo that Mary had*
> *With me, the other night,*
> *Was intimate and personal,*
> *And,— well, you know all right!*
>
> *The huzzlecoo her father had*
> *With me, soon after that,*
> *Was intimate and personal —*
> *I left without my hat!*

Hy′gog, *n.*   1. An unsatisfied desire.   2. An anxious suspense.

Hy-gog′i-cal, *a.*   Unattainable; next to impossible.

Oh, that hygogical curtain-shade that simply will *not* catch, jiggle it up and down as you will!   Oh, that mirror, too high for you, even on tiptoe!   Oh, that telephone operator who won't answer — and that match you can't find, in the dark. Hygogs.   Did you ever wait for a sneeze that wouldn't come?   It is a hygog.

The chandelier — just out of reach; with lighted match, how often have I striven to light the gas!   It was a hygog. How near, and yet how far!

Your note paper too large for the envelope.   Fold it over on the edges and cram it in —   No, it sticks, and will not go!   It's a hygog.   Or, if once rammed in, no man can draw it forth.   (See *Wijjicle.*)

Ah, but you suffer, not only for your hygog, but for another's: The actor, who forgets his lines, the parlor elocutionist who pauses and cannot get the next verse — the hygog is an agony unendurable.   (See *Splooch.*)

Hygogical is the strained anxiety of one who waits in nervous suspense for someone to meet her at the station in time to catch the train.

The cave-man knew it when, pursued by a saber-toothed tiger, he crawled out on the end of a too slender limb.

In Baltimore an oyster rare
   Lay on his shell of pearl,
Huge as an alligator pear —
   'Twas placed before a girl.

Two times to swallow it she tried,
   Three times, and still did fail;
The hygog was too long, too wide —
   Let's kindly draw the veil!

40

Hyp′ri-jimp, *n.* 1. A man in a woman's place or who does women's work. 2. An obedient and thoroughly domesticated husband. 3. A man entirely surrounded by women.

He may wash the dishes because his wife is ill, or because she is making a speech on the street corner; but he is still a hyprijimp. He may wheel the baby-carriage because he is in love with his offspring or afraid of his wife; he is a hyprijimp. (See *Vorge.*)

He who carries bundles, kisses his wife in public, does errands for his sister or criticises hats with real fervor is a hyprijimp.

The hyprijimp is the male guest at a woman's club; a man at a prayer meeting, an author who reads his own poems, a non-smoker, a husband in an employment agency. (See *Varm.*)

The husband of a Suffragette is a hyprijimp. (See *Wowze.*)

Within a tea-room, pink and dim,
Mid candlesticks and tiles,
A hyprijimp, the only Him,
Was waiting, wreathed in smiles.

Ah, did he swear at Her delay?
Did rage his forehead crimp?
Oh, no, he was not built that way;
He was a hyprijimp!

Ig′moil, *n.*   1.   A quarrel over money matters;
a sordid dispute.   2. The driving of a hard
bargain; a petty law suit.

Before the funeral was over, the brothers and sisters were
fighting over the will; yes, before the father was dead, they
had their igmoils over the property.

Woe to the wife of the stingy husband!   Many are her
igmoils.   (See *Hyprijimp.*)

And yet no one can escape the igmoil when abroad.   When
they charge you, as an American, four times the price, how
can you help trying to jew them down?   (See *Jurp.*)

The igmoil is the pawnbroker's daily bread.

To lose a friend through an igmoil, is the most sordid
tragedy of life.

> *My wife had bought a summer hat;*
>   *It cost her 19.20,*
> *That is, of course, it cost* me *that.*
>   *I thought 6.50 plenty.*
>
> *We had an igmoil, for, you see,*
>   *I had to have that money.*
> *She couldn't see I needed three*
>   *New golf clubs! Ain't that funny?*

Imp'kin, *n.*   A superhuman pet; a human offspring masquerading in the form of a beast;
an animal that is given overabundant care.

The impkin is the sole heir of Race Suicide, his mother being The High Cost of Living.   He is supposed to "love his
mummy."

Impkins are canine and feline, but their parents are usually
asinine.

The impkin is hyper-domesticated but doesn't particularly
like it.   An impkin being frankly natural is always a shock
to his mistress.   (See *Frowk.*)

The impkin is particularly affected by large blondes, and
always when their hair is hennaed.

Impkins have collars but no cuffs.   They wear boots and
ulsters and live in limousines.   They give teas and grudg-
ingly tolerate the presence of the master of the family.   (See
Varm.)

The impkin is supposed to have all of a baby's virtues and
none of his faults.   It requires more care, but doesn't jeopard
one's place in Society.

> *An impkin, noble and refined,*
>   *Complained, " No doubt you see,*
> *Of course, I do not have to mind*
>   *My mistress — she minds me."*
>
> *" A Pomeranian canine, I,—*
>   *She's but a common woman;*
> *She's really quite insulting — why,*
>   *She seems to think I'm human! "*

I'o-bink, *n.*   1. An unplaceable resemblance; an uncertain similarity.   2. An inaccessible memory.   3. An unexplainable sound.

A flash of mysterious semi-recognition confuses you for a moment.   "Where — when — have I done just that thing before?"   No use to search your memory or puzzle your wits; you can never catch up with the elusive thought: It's an iobink.

That strangely familiar face you pass in the street — the figure you dimly recognize in the restaurant.

The iobink, like a will-o'-the-wisp, leads you on in fond pursuit.   It was probably some clerk in a dry-goods store, or the assistant in the grocery.   (See *Oofle.*)

So the iobink subtly tortures you.   You hear its human voice in sounds of running water, or the moan of the wind. And, as you lie in bed, terrified, an unexplainable noise keeps you awake.   But, it's nothing — only an iobink.

What *is* that word, that you cannot quite remember?   It circles above your head, just out of reach.   The iobink will not come, except uncalled.   The tune you strive to bring back haunts you like a ghost.   You cannot give it audible form.   It hovers beyond your consciousness in a world of iobinks.   (See *Rizgidget.*)

> *Who was she?   And what was her name?*
> *Somehow, I couldn't think.*
> *Why was my memory so to blame?*
> *It was an iobink.*
>
> *Where had I seen that face, that stare?*
> *In some old, previous life?*
> *The iobink dissolved — and there*
> *She was — my former wife!*

Jip, *n.* 1. A dangerous topic of conversation;
 2. A suggestive remark.
Jip'lish, *a.* Likely to lead to an explosion; too
personal.

Never make fun of Reno — even to Mrs. Newlywed — she may have a ticket already bought, and it will be a jip. (See *Pooje.*)

Never speak slightingly of actors, dentists, Jews, Socialists, mothers-in-law, plumbers, Christian Scientists or Progressives — the man in the embroidered velvet necktie who has begun to glare at you, may be all of them — it's a jip.

Did you ever ask a grey-gowned brunette the whereabouts of her husband only to find that he had died last week? Rather jiplish!

Anyway, you're pretty sure to make a jip with your girl, sooner or later — whether you discuss her best hat or her best friend, the talk is apt to be jiplish. To ask a woman her age is a jip.

Never ask a man what his wife said when he got home late — it's a jip. (See *Skyscrimble.*)

> *I asked Bill Green how Mrs. Green*
> *Enjoyed her motor trip,*
> *And if she liked their limousine —*
> *Believe me, 'twas a jip!*
>
> *It was a jip to talk of her,*
> *For she eloped last fall;*
> *She ran away with his chauffeur,*
> *And took him, car and all!*

Jir′ri-wig, *n.* 1. A superficial traveler. 2. The Philistine abroad. 3. A bromide in search of himself.
Jir′ri-wig, *v.* To travel with one's eyes shut. To destroy opportunity.

I met Mrs. Jirriwig first in Paris. She had been there three months, and had spent 87 days with modistes and lingeristes, one day at the Louvre — the rest of the time she had been ill. When she wasn't trying on gowns, she was in a cab, going to or from the process. (See *Mooble.*)

Later, on the train, I met Mr. Jirriwig, on the way to Venice. The train flew by the bounteous beauties of Lombardy, historic and picturesque. Did Mr. Jirriwig look out of the window? No, he was too busy reading his Baedeker, learning about Venice. In Venice, he spent his time in gondolas, reading up Florence. In Florence he sat at little café tables, turning the pages of his red-covered book and getting acquainted with Rome. So he saw Europe,— in type.

But there are thousands of Jirriwigs in Paris. They have been there for years, and all the French they know is *"Combien?"* They are in a state of perpetual disgust, that things are so different to anything in the United States.

But there are Jirriwigs in New York also. They live in the Subway, in offices and in flats. (See *Cowcat.*)

> Said Mr. Jirriwig, one day,
>   To Mrs. Jirriwig,
> *"Let's see the Versailles fountains play;
>   They say they're fine and big!"*
>
> *" Yes,"* said his wife, *" they're fine and big,*
>   *I've seen them once, you know!"*
> *" Thank God!"* said Mr. Jirriwig,
>   *" Then I won't have to go!"*

JIRRIWIG

Ju′jasm, *n.* 1. A much-needed relief; a long-desired satisfaction. 2. An expansion of sudden joy.

Ju-jas′mic, *a.* Offering relief from suffering, or an escape from ennui.

Thank God the train has started! So, after the long, dreary wait on a side-track, your heart expands in a delicious jujasm. As noise after long silence, so is silence after much noise, a jujasm. (See *Gollohix.*)

After your slow recovery, jujasmic is the doctor's dictum, " I think we'll have to get you up tomorrow."

Why is Helen's face with wild jujasm alight? Dilatory Dick has at last proposed. (See *Xenogore.*)

As deep as the grim horror of the dentist's deed, just so high does your spirit rise in jujasm when the tooth is out.

Spring! After the long suspense is over, the first day of balm and warmth brings jujasm to your heart.

As a hot drink on a sleigh-ride; as food after a long fast — so is the first sight of women to a sailor, after his eighteen months at sea, jujasmic.

Last night, I took high-browed Harriet to the theatre, and she talked of her soul, while I perished. Oh, the rise of the curtain on that third act of farcical folly! It was a jujasm. (See *Orobaldity.*)

> *Jujasmic is it when, at night,*
> *Your baby stops his wails;*
> *Or when the land, at last in sight,*
> *The seasick traveller hails.*
>
> *But what are such jujasms to this —*
> *(I hope your memory's strong,)*
> *That first ecstatic, rapturous kiss*
> *You waited for, so long!*

Jul'lix, *n.*   A mental affinity, with a similar taste and inclination.   2. One who knew you when you were a child.

"He speaks my own language!" Smile if you will, and call it sentimentality, but some there are, your jullixes, who laugh at the same jokes as you and weep at the same sights. Out of the ruck of social five-o'clocks you pick them, like single pearls out of dead oysters, and they shine in your memory forever. Three words spoken, and you know them as you know yourself; and you have floated lightly from ports of conventionality, never to return. (See *Frime.*)

Such is your jullix. It is not only that he loves your authors and your songs; not that he has been to the same queer foreign little towns that you have "discovered"— or even that she has had the same operation. Of your jullix you know far more than that — you know his soul.

When you are rich, sedate and prominent, comes one with whiskers and calls you, "Bill!" He knew you when you wore short trousers; and he, too, knows your language — that all but forgotten speech of your youth. (See *Thusk.*)

Is she a jullix who was once engaged to the man whom you have married? A jullix? Yes, but alas, she knows too much for friendship!

A woman's jullix is one who knows her real age.

> *How Elsie stared!   Did Elsie guess*
> *What bond united her*
> *To that girl opposite her?   Yes!*
> *It was her jullix, sure.*

> *Oh, not from souls akin, and less*
> *From friendship did she know her;*
> *But both had bought the self-same dress*
> *In the same department store!*

Jurp, *n.* 1. A haughty inferior; a saucy underling. 2. An impudent servant or clerk.
Jur'pid, *a.* Insubordinate or impertinent.

Cooks, brakemen, shop girls are often jurpid. The whis-
tling, gum-chewing office boy, who won't take in your card and
says, "The manager's out," is jurpid.

The officious policeman, the barber who talks, the head-
waiter, who always gives you the table you don't want, is
jurpid when you object. (See *Moosoo.*)

What good does it do to report the jurp? You'll only
have on your conscience the fact that a man with a
big family has lost his job. And so, you swallow his jurpid
jibes.

"Well," says the jurpid milliner, "you *said* you wanted
a red hat, and this hat's red. We ain't got anything *redder.*
If I'd a-known you wanted *blue,* why didn't you say so, and
I'd a-shown you some purple ones! You can see for yourself green's more becoming, though."

Colored maids, messenger boys and janitors cannot help
being jurps — they were born that way. (See *Splooch.*)

> *It was a jurp who answered back,*
> *Impertinent and pert;*
> *A filthy beast, who drove a hack —*
> *You should have seen his shirt!*
>
> *And I a gentleman! Whee-ew,*
> *What jurpid things he said!*
> *I'd given him a dollar, too!*
> *But it was made of lead.*

Kid'loid, *n.* 1. A precocious or self-assertive infant; an *enfant terrible.* 2. A hotel or stage child. Any juvenile person who is too ubiquitous.

Kid'loid, *a.* Impertinent or offensive, in a childish way.

In the hotel the kidloid is manufactured and developed from shy and timid modesty to the final perfect stages of conspicuous vulgarity. He is like an improbable old man, or a cynical hag but without the charm of age.

The kidloid, in comic papers, hides under the couch when his sister's beau is calling, and is subsequently bribed to silence. In actual life, however, he is much more offensive when you know he's about. (See *Vorge.*)

The kidloid is called upon to recite " pieces " before company, and invariably makes a fool of his parents.

The kidloid makes conversation an agony, and has the apparent power of a multiple personality. He seems like at least a dozen persons when he is in the room.

Kidloids are created by fond and idolatrous parents by the simple process of giving them their own way.

The stage kidloid is a cross between an intelligent ape and a mummy. The hotel kidloid is an anthropoid dynamo. (See *Gollohix.*)

The kidloid at the Beach Hotel
We thought a model child,
For he behaved so very well —
He was so meek and mild.

But every girl, for comfort's sake,
Had paid him, every day
That she had company, to make
That kidloid stay away!

KIPE

Kipe, *v.*   To inspect critically; to appraise prag-
matically; to eye with jealousy or envy.
Kipe, *n.*   A woman's glance at another woman.

Up and down, from hat to heel, women kipe each other
insolently as they pass.   In subway or in street-car, every
woman who enters is kiped by her shrewd-eyed sisters.   In
that keen first glance, every article of the new comer's rai-
ment is appraised.   (See *Flooijab.*)

So, at the employment agency, the housewife kipes the
cook, and cook kipes housewife, each turning away with the
thought, "She won't do for me."   (See *Snosh.*)

Employer kipes the applicant for position, accepts or re-
jects.   The poker-player, with his last blue chip in the pot,
kipes his four-card draw.   The fastidious smoker kipes the
gift cigar.   The golfer kipes his " lie."

Says Aunt Samanthy Hanks to Mary Jane at the county
fair, as she kipes the patchwork bedquilts in the gallery,
" Mine's better'n her'n."   Says the mother of the bride, as
she kipes the wedding presents spread out on the table,
" H'm! his folks must be close-fisted."   (See *Gefoojet.*)

As you whiz, motoring through the park, a car flashes by
— but not too fast for your automobile host to kipe it:
" 1913 36-6 ' Strangler '—   No good! "

So do the village girls kipe the strange young man in town.

> *Carlotta kipes at Ermyntrude,*
> *And Ermyntrude at Rose;*
> *And every stitch that each has on*
> *Each other lady knows.*

> *Each lady knows the other's faults,*
> *Her quality and size,*
> *And just how old and good she is;*
> *Would men were half as wise!*

Krip′sle, *n.* A worrying physical sensation, an
invisible annoyance absorbing one's attention.
Krip′sly, *a.* Distracting, distrait, unmentiona-
bly provocative.

Walking on spilt sugar is kripsly.

That fugitive morsel of walnut-meat in the cavity of your
bi-cuspid, which your tongue chases so thoughtfully, but
in vain — a fascinating kripsle, as kripsly as a loose tooth!
(See *Vorge.*)

Has a hairpin fallen down your back? Smile, and don't
be kripsly; beware that faraway look that tells the story!
And when through that hole in your stocking your big toe
sticks out, don't be kripsled!

The ancient Stoics, like the modern Christian Scientists,
declared that all kripsles were Error. But Mortal Mind
knows full well that when you have both hands and arms full
of bundles, the drop that hangs, pulling at the end of your
nose, is a kripsle hard to bear — it cannot be snuffed in or
shaken off.

The philosopher may be calm, even while his foot is
awakening from a sound sleep; the poet may not lose his
inspiration even with a hair in his mouth; but to plain John
W. Smith, of 101 Eighth Avenue, a kripsle is as disturbing
as a broken elbow, or a bleeding poached egg in its death
agony. (See *Slub.*)

Perhaps you think that smile you caught,
Her introspective air,
Her pensive mien — is caused by thought
Too shy for you to share.

Ah, so it is! With all your tact
You fail. It is no use!
For she is kripsled by the fact
That her left garter's loose.

Lal′li-fac-tion, *n.* A verbose story, a joke repeated.
Lal′li-fy, *v.* 1. To act too slowly; to delay.
2. To give an over-painstaking or super-elaborate performance.

Did you ever hear an Englishman lallify his conversation with, "What I mean to say is this," and "if you know what I mean" and "do you see"? So the shop girl lallifies her talk with "Listen here!" or "Say, listen!" while she gropes for an idea. The preacher, barren of fresh thoughts, lallifies his meager sermon. "Fourthly, beloved brethren —" (See *Drillig.*)

A "talky" play is lallified till the house walks out. Like a song sung too slowly, so is the lallified talk of the young man who doesn't want to escort that particular girl home. (See *Vorge* and *Xenogore.*)

The lallified book: Wide, wide margins and thick, thick paper — or, maybe it is lallified only with adjectives or adverbs.

Have you ever heard that man Gerrish tell his favorite story, lallifying it with dialect-dialogue till you yawned? Then, after you have forced a laugh, he lallifies the point with reminiscent unction, repeating it reflectively, itching for more applause.

The consummate lallification is two women saying goodbye to each other. (See *Wumgush.*)

For months and months the Hemmingways
Have lallified of Baby,
How Baby walks and talks and plays —
And have I listened? Maybe.

But now the time has come, today,
To lallify that pair;
For I am working on a play,
And talk about it there!

Le′o-lump, *n.* 1. An interrupter of conversations; one who always brings the talk back to himself. 2. An egoist; one who thinks you are necessarily interested in what interests him.

"When I was in Italy," I began, carelessly —
"Oh, dear, I've never been out of New York!" she whined.
"I do wish I could go to Italy sometime!"
She was a leolump. I could not mention anything without her applying it to herself. The word "objective" was not in her dictionary.

The leolump always caps your story with one stranger and bigger than yours. He has acquired the art of the superlative. (See *Persotude.*)

Talk to a leolump actor of logarithms, and in an instant he will prove relationship; he can show himself to be first cousin to the carbo-hydrates in a congress of foreign chemists.

Conversation? Impossible when a leolump is present. Even if he has the civility not to interrupt, which he hasn't, the minute you stop speaking he is astride his hobby and riding himself to social suicide. (See *Blurb.*)

He has a million subjects ready in the pigeon-hole marked "I."

Women are seldom leolumps, for they never allow the conversation to depart from the subject of themselves. And so they never have to interrupt, or bring the topic back.

He breaks into your talk, and cries,
"Oh, that reminds me,"— then
Oh, how his tale your patience tries!
But you begin again.

A leolump you cannot shame;
His head is like a fly's;
His brain is small, but all the same,
He has a thousand "I's,"

Loob'lum, *n.*   1. A pleasant thing that is bad for one; rich, but dangerous food.   2. A flatterer; flattery.

Loob'loid, *a.*   1. Sweet, but indigestible.

Loobloid is the broiled live lobster and the hot mince pie. Loobloid, ice water when you are warm and whiskey when you are cold.

But human nature still woos the looblum. For youthful inexperience, green apples and the first cigar; for age, ennui and discouragement,— opium, morphine and cocaine.

Yes, all those things of which the bromide says, " I like them, but they don't like me," are loobloid. Black coffee at night and a cocktail in the morning — both are looblums.

And yet, the mental looblums are worse; corroding the character with sweetest poisons. How rapturously we gulp them down! You ask criticism on what you know is bad, and enjoy the loobloid praise. On his opening night, the ambitious playwright makes his speech in answer to the looblums of applause. (See *Wumgush.*)

On the morning after her wedding-day, the blue-nosed bride reads loobloid descriptions of her beauty at the ceremony.

Most loobloid, but most sweet! The flattery of the fond and doting parent. (See *Culp.*)

> *My after-dinner speech was lame,*
>   *No gift of gab is mine;*
> *The chairman praised me, all the same,*
>   *He said my talk was fine.*
>
> *I had been terrified, and I*
>   *Made blunders that were frightful;*
> *The chairman lied — but what's a lie?*
>   *His looblum was delightful!*

Ma-chiz′zlum, *n.* 1. A thinly disguised boredom. 2. A disappointing spectacle. 3. The
apotheosis of the obvious.
Ma-chiz′zle, *v.* 1. To attempt unsuccessfully to
please. 2. To try too hard to like something.

Pageants, processions and picnics are all machizzlums; for
well you know before they start, that boredom shall be yours.
Why does one stand jammed, crowded, uncomfortable, peer-
ing over bobbing heads at men in curious costumes marching
by? Why endure the long waits of the machizzlum? After
it is over, one wonders why he has just consented to be
machizzled.

Almost every motion picture show is a machizzlum to sane-
brained folk. So is watching the election returns, or an automobile race where there are no accidents, or a partial eclipse
of the moon.

Do you call upon a belle? Do you try to converse with
the " popular " man? Surely you will be machizzled. Don't
try to read the book that has been too widely praised; what
everyone likes, is sure to be a machizzlum. (See *Ovotch.*)

The easiest way to be machizzled, is to fall in love with an
actress.

The young, young girl smirks and smiles and blushing,
says: "O Mr. Poet, tell me, when did you first find you
had this power?" But to the less sentimental herd, the great
machizzlum is to be introduced to a celebrity. (See *Yowf.*)

It costs you ten to see the sight,
  The weather always lowers;
Your seat is narrow, hard and tight,
  You wait for hours and hours;

And when at last the thing is o'er,
  And the last red light has fizzled
You know the thing has been a bore;
  Once more you've been machizzled!

Meem, *n.* An artificial half light that women
love; a charitable obscurity; a becoming gloom.
Meem′y, *a.* Obscure, dim, uncertain.

From a brilliantly lighted hall outside, you plunge into the
meemy parlors wherein shadows flit, vague, uncertain. You
stumble over a rug. A silhouette rises and comes forth to
meet you. How many are there 'there? Who are they?
Mysterious is the meem!

Meemy is that uneasy, tantalizing obscurity, that depressed
semi-darkness that women who-would-be-artistic find so necessary for the preservation of their charms. To a man the
meem is maddening and meaningless; if there are pretty
women present, he wishes to see them. (See *Kipe.*)

There's a dim, religious meem, the shadowy penumbra of
grcat cathedrals — the sentimental meem, the sad gloom
of the funeral — the amorous meem, the starlit darkness,
wherein lovers linger.

The meemy woman always sits with her back to the light,
to watch you from an ambush. (See *Squinch.*)

Candles are meemy, especially red ones — except when
used properly, in clusters.

Still, a meem does keep out the flies.

> All meemy was the studio,
>   And meemy maidens — wait!
> Say, were they maidens? Heavens, no!
>   Are maidens thirty-eight?
>
> Well, anyway, they passed for such,
>   For candles make a meem
> That women think disguises much.
>   Things are not what they seem.

Moo′ble, *n.* 1. A mildly amusing affair; a
moderate success. 2. A person or thing over
whom it is difficult to be enthusiastic.
Moo′bly, *adj., adv.* Innocuous, feebly, without uction.

The Samoans have a word which means, " A-party-is-
approaching-which-contains-neither-a-clever-man-nor-a-pretty-
woman." It's a mooble. Dancing with your own wife is a
mooble — a fairly good play, a dinner-party where the *ménu*
makes up for the *dramatis personæ* — moobles!
Mooble is the word that " Damns with faint praise "— an
" awfully nice girl "— why not say it point blank: " She's
a mooble." (See *Cowcat.*)
Thanksgiving dinner in a restaurant — a mooble.
A tame young man — a mooble. (See *Snosh.*)
You may be a wonder with women,— leaving a trail of
fire behind you as you go — but you're a mooble at tennis.
You're a mooble at pool, too, although you " used to play a
very good game."
Moobly novels are written by — well, of course you know
already. Moobly foods: cornstarch custard, warm iced tea,
vanilla ice cream. The W.C.T.U. is a mooble. So is a com-
mencement essay, and most tall, blonde women.
But the perfect mooble is the man you used to be engaged
to. (See *Thusk.*)

At first I thought her a genius bright,
Almost an angel — out of sight!
But the second time that I went to call
I found her a mooble, after all.

Only a mooble, and then she wrote,
Oh, what a moobly, moobly note!
And how can you wonder my love should end?
She began her letter to me, " Dear Friend "!

Moo'soo, *a.* 1. Sulky, out of sorts, blue, taciturn, discontented. 2. Unsuccessful; getting
out of order; going wrong, delayed.

Moosoo is a mild form of " the dumps." You are moosoo
while waiting for someone who is late, especially late for dinner; when your dress doesn't quite fit, or isn't quite becoming.

Moosoo is the secondary stage of getting over acute ill
humor. It is the mood of the wife in her second year of
marriage.

Moosoo is the clerk who is discontented with his position.
Moosoo is the salesman, when you return goods or exchange
them. (See *Jurp*.)

Moosoo is the brakeman, when the train is delayed.

The wall-flower at the dance is moosoo, though her smiles
are pungent.

Moosoo is the maiden when the young man fails to propose,
although she shows it not.

Moosoo is the interested escort, when the restaurant music
is too loud at dinner. (See *Huzzlecoo*.)

Children are moosoo, when they can't go to the circus; the
traveling salesman, when his cigar leaks; and even the polite
husband, when the burned chops are set before him.

The weather, itself, can be moosoo, with clouds and dull-
ness for weeks at a time.

> *The day was moosoo; Mary Ann*
> *Was moosoo, so was I;*
> *And moosoo were the girl and man*
> *Whom we'd invited — why?*
>
> *Why did we sulk, disgusted, far*
> *From home, discouraged, blue?*
> *Because my brand new motor-car*
> *Alas, was moosoo, too!*

Nink, *n.*   1. A useless " antique " object, pre-
served in worship of the picturesque.   2. An
imitation of a by-gone style.
Nink′ty, *a.*   Architecturally dishonest.

You buy your ninks at " Ye Olde Shoppe " and by that
" Ye "— you shall know the ninkty.   For a nink is a brass
candlestick with no candle in it; the pewter mugs and plat-
ters, unpolished, on the sideboard; the old china, dusty and
unused upon the wall; old tiles and brass knockers.

The old flax-wheel in the corner is a nink; the framed old
sporting prints of horse races and stagecoaches; the framed
theatre bills.   Pompeian bronze tripods, never lighted, in
hotel corridors.   (See *Gorgule*.)

A beefsteak party is a nink, and May-day dances and
pageants; anything revived, revamped for modern use.
Doors, covered with nails and decorative hinges bolted on;
things sewed with thongs; imitation parchment scrolls.
Whale-oil lamps, ships' lanterns; almost any object of leather,
copper, or brass.   (See *Gefoojet*.)

Architectural ninks are imitation beams in the ceiling; hol-
low columns; furniture, with imitation mortises and pegs.

The ninkiest nink of all is the framed motto on the wall,
or a legend painted over the fireplace.

> *The ninks that Mr. Parvenu*
>   *Has bought, because " artistic,"*
> *Are " genuine antiques," though you*
>   *Call them anachronistic.*

> *But still, one nink is not disgraced —*
>   *That sun dial he got*
> *Is now appropriately placed;*
>   *He put it on his yacht!*

Nodge, *n.* 1. The only one of its kind or set.
2. A person who doesn't " fit in; " a Martian.
Nod'gy, *a.* 1. Impertinent, inconsistent, in-
applicable; having no mate.

Wife or housewife — all women know the nodge. It's the
odd tumbler, or odd plate,— the one button whose mates have
disappeared; the one glove that persistently turns up; the
single shoe or stocking; those three trading-stamps she
doesn't throw away.

Nodgy is that extra envelope — too small for the paper;
the one chair that doesn't match the furniture; the lone coat,
whose skirt has long since worn out; the hat that goes with
no possible gown.

Nodgy is the Methodist minister at a poker party; nodgy
the cut-up at prayer meeting, or the ugly damsel at the ball.

The modest country girl is nodgy with women who smoke
cigarettes. (See *Ovotch.*)

How long have you saved that old lace yoke — waiting for
something to put it on. Throw it away! It's a nodge. (See
Gefoojet.)

> *I took my aunt to see the town,*
> *A task I couldn't dodge;*
> *At every cabaret she'd frown,*
> *She was a perfect nodge.*

> *But when, to visit her, I went*
> *To Pudding Centre, Mass.,*
> *She took me to a gospel tent,*
> *I was a nodge, alas!*

Nul'kin, *n.* 1. The core or inside history of any occurrence. A true, but secret explanation. 2. Facts known, but not told.

The " nigger-in-the-woodpile " was named Mr. Nulkin.
The object of a trial by jury is to find the nulkin of the crime.
Why were they divorced? What does she see in him? Nobody knows the nulkin. It is the skeleton in the closet.
The nulkin is the true motive. *Cherchez la nulkin.*
The diplomatic service is full of nulkins.
Why didn't we go to war with Mexico? Did we fear Japan? What is the nulkin?
Why did she get the part of leading lady? This is the theatrical nulkin.
Why is a book popular? Publishers strive in vain to discover the literary nulkin. (See *Edicle.*)
Why do imitators fail? Because they copy outside traits, and not the inmost nulkin. (See *Bripkin.*)
A nulkin is the secret thought you never tell,— the *real* reason why your wife doesn't like Sarah.

" What does he see in her? " we ask;
" What does she see in him? "
Ah, matrimonial nulkins task
The brains of seraphim!

The nulkin is what you have tried,
And I have tried to know;
Instead, we judge from what's outside —
Perhaps 'tis better so.

Oo′fle, *n.* 1. A person whose name you cannot remember. 2. A state of forgetfulness regarding a friend or thing.

Oo′fle, *v.* 1. To try to find out a person's name without asking. 2. To talk to an unknown person without introducing him to a nearby friend.

Oofled, *p.p.* Mortified needlessly.

"How do you do, Mr. Goheevus; you don't remember me, do you?" Are you oofled? If you are not, you will say, "No, why should I?" But alas, one usually *is* oofled, and struggles desperately to conceal the fact, groping wildly in the well of one's memory for the lost name, while one's friends stand about reproachfully, waiting to be introduced.

Any person whose name is Baker is an oofle,— or Brown, or Davis. The other most celebrated oofles are Harris, Johnson, Miller, Palmer, Pratt, Porter, Stevens, Simpson, Richards, Roberts, Taylor, Wheeler and Wilson. Can you ever tell one from another? No, not even if the pistol is held to your head! (See *Iobink*.)

Of course what's an oofle to you may not be oofly to me, especially if my name is Goheevus. (See *Mooble*.) But everyone is oofled by a hostess who mumbles her introductions. (See *Cowcat*.)

> *No wonder I was oofled, for,*
> *Although I knew his face,*
> *In some way, for the life of me,*
> *His name I couldn't place;*
>
> *Now, was it Harris, Johnson, Brown,*
> *Or Palmer, Jones or Platt?*
> *He was an Oofle, anyway —*
> *There was no doubt of that!*

O-ro-bal′di-ty, *n.*   1. Modern witchcraft; Orientalism adapted to Occidental intellects; Emerson-and-milk.   2. An alleged process of getting wise quickly; a short cut to success.

Orobaldity in its most acute form, *i. e.,* Vedantic philosophy with the asceticism left out, is particularly affected by females who are not willing to gain success or happiness through mere effort. It consists of gambling with the intellect, in order to gain a dishonest percentage of mental profit.

Orobaldity is, in the main, a modern magic supposed to be controlled by cryptic phrases and abracadabra such as " into the silence " and " holding the thought." It is not necessary to know the esoteric meaning of such charms, or to exert any actual energy in obtaining one's desires. (See *Gubble.*)

Orobaldity is a thing of " vibrations " and " thought currents " and is founded mainly upon analogies with wireless telegraphy and other modern scientific discoveries. It finds occult meanings in colors and numbers.

Orobaldity is medieval mysticism, mainly practised by women who have nothing else to do. (See *Mooble.*)

Actresses out of work find in orobaldity a good substitute for trying to get an engagement. Neurotic and erotic temperaments find it an admirable stimulant to egoism.

> *First she was a Christian Scientist,*
>   *And then a New Thought daughter;*
> *Next she became a Theosophist,*
>   *Then Bahaïism caught her.*
>
> *But now her Occultism wanes,*
>   *Astrology dispelling;*
> *Her Orobaldity remains*
>   *As just plain Fortune-Telling.*

O'votch, *n.*   1. One who does things merely because others do.   One swayed by popular crazes, the victim of custom.   2. A currently popular fad or form of amusement.

To-day, baseball is an ovotch; dancing, whist, golf, Eurythmics, Eugenics, Kelly pool and Burgess Unabridged. (See *Blurb.*)

Golf is a re-ovotch, a revival of an obsolete sport. The popular tune of the day is an ovotch; the current slang; the fad of the hour in custom and costume.

Past is the ovotch of the bicycle, croquet and archery; to-morrow the ovotch may be put upon flying, skin-tight trousers, or free love.   (See *Thusk.*)

One ovotch will never be revived, the family reciter, with her vox humana tremulo voice.

> *In Grandma's time, the ovotch quaint*
> *Was to be meek and modest;*
> *She used to have the " vapors "—(faint)*
> *She was so tightly bodiced.*
>
> *What is the ovotch for a maid*
> *To-day?   The gown that lets*
> *Her lissome figure be displayed,—*
> *And smoking cigarettes.*

> **Pa-loo′dle,** *n.* One who gives unnecessary or undesired information. 2. Uncalled-for advice. 3. A recital of obvious details.
> **Pa-loo′dle,** *v.* To give the above; to assume omniscience.
> **Pa-loo′dlum.** A paloodle talk.

Have you ever in the theatre sat in front of a gabby gent, who paloodles his girl with the story of the play, announcing each entrance and exit?

The paloodle is ubiquitous; at the baseball game, he explains each play; at the pool-table, he tells you what you ought to do, or should have done. He is proficient in the knowledge of how to run other people's business. (See *Drillig*.)

Old maids paloodle you with advice on how to train your children, or how to manage a husband. (See *Lallify*.)

A horse falls on the slippery pavement. Immediately it is surrounded with paloodles, suggesting blankets, and straps and buckles, and "Sit on its head." It's the paloodle's head that should be sat upon.

The stage manager paloodles the actor: "You cross here," he says; and, "You want to cry all through that scene." No wonder the dramatic critic also paloodles the actor on the opening night. (See *Yowf* and *Edicle*.)

Paloodling the baby is the favorite occupation of the second year of married life. "How to cure a cold," a paloodlum in six parts.

> *Each base was full, the score was tied,*
> *The strikes they numbered two;*
> *Still that paloodle at my side*
> *Paloodled me and you!*
>
> *The inning was the ninth, alas,*
> *But the end I did not see —*
> *For I was murdering the ass*
> *Who'd been paloodling me!*

Paw'dle, *n.* 1. One who is vicariously famous,
   rich or influential. 2. A person of mediocre
   ability, raised to undeserved prominence.
Paw'dle, *v.* To wear another's clothes.

You all know him, the pawdle, or her, who pawdles in un-
paid-for prosperity.

The husband of the famous wife, or the wife of a Star.

The child of a celebrity; the daughter of a president.
(See *Yowf.*)

The editor of an Anthology, or a translator. An adopted
child. A woman with dyed hair. An officer of the militia.
An American countess. The author of a privately printed
book. (See *Edicle.*)

To pawdle is to go to the theatre on passes; to ride in
other people's automobiles, to use hotel or club stationcry.

To pawdle is the poor husband of the rich wife; also the
husband of the industrious vaudeville artiste, or the farmer,
who lets Florrie do all the work, while he talks politics at
the village store. (See *Hyprijimp.*)

Behold Brother Pawdle, the Past Grand Worthy Superior
Thingamajig, of the Glorified Order of Pawdles, in his
transcendental uniform and gold sword! He is really the
book-keeper of a fish-shop.

> *Only a pawdle — don't tell her so,*
>   *For she thinks, as pawdles do,*
> *She is sought because of herself, you know;*
>   *But you know that that isn't true.*

> *Only a pawdle — but never mind,*
>   *For she'll die in due season, when*
> *Her proper place she will really find —*
>   *Not even a pawdle, then!*

71

Per′so-tude, *n.*   Social warmth, personal magnetism, charm.
Per′so-mag, *n.*   The unit of social favor.

A man charged to the highest voltage of persotude could
borrow any amount of money.   The charge fluctuates in the
same person.   After a good dinner, one vibrates sometimes
up to 7,000 persomags.   Cocktails, compliments and social
success make one buzz with persotude.   (See *Gubble.*)
Anyone troubled with negative persotude should take a
rest cure and test his recovery by trying to sell life insurance, which requires the greatest sparking charge.   (See
Spuzz.)
Persotude is independent of beauty, though it is hard to
make a woman believe it.   Getting rich adds to one's persotude,— but not always.   Rockefeller's persotude is less than
6½ persomags.   (See *Yowf.*)
Nicknames are prime evidence of rich persotude.
The highest persomags in America are Roosevelt, Christie
Matthewson and Maude Adams.

> *When Walter, at his Sunday School*
>   *Declaimed " The Old Front Gate,"*
> *They flattered so the little fool*
>   *His persotude was great.*

> *He went upon the stage and planned*
>   *To be a tragic hero,*
> *He never even got a " hand "—*
>   *His persotude was zero.*

Pooje, *n.* 1. An embarrassing situation; a sense of guilt; a regrettable discovery. 2. One who is caught in the act.

Pooje, *v.* To make a painful discovery; unwittingly to create a scene.

Poojed, *p.p.* Disconcerted, mortified, aghast.

A pooje is a sudden desire to become invisible; as when, entertaining company, the neat housewife sees a cockroach crawl along the floor.

John was kissing Mary, when Eliza opened the door. It was a pooje. John and Mary were poojed good. But even this wasn't as bad as when John tried to kiss Eliza. She poojed him. "Sir!" she said, "how *dare* you?"

Last night I dreamed that I was standing on the corner of Forty-second Street and Broadway at 10-45 P. M. just as the theatre crowd swept by. Yes, of course you know the sensation well — I was in my night-gown, with bare feet! Was I poojed? Rath-*er!* (See *Agowilt.*)

Also, you can get poojed merely by trying to step up a top stair which doesn't happen to be there, or by being caught putting one cent in the contribution-plate.

Never listen at the keyhole when a man and his wife are quarreling inside; he may suddenly open the door and pooje you. (See *Bimp.*)

> *Said Parks to his stenographer,*
> *"All ready? Well, take this!"*
> *And then Parks gave the girl a hug,*
> *And then gave her a kiss.*
>
> *Just then the door was opened wide,*
> *And his surprise was huge —*
> *'Twas Parks's wife; he nearly died,*
> *For Parks was in a pooje!*

Quink, *n.*   1. An expression or mood of anxious expectancy; absorbed determination.
Quinked, *p.p.*   Haggardly resolute, with the excitement of suspense.
Quink'y, *a.*   Tense, uncertain, fearful.

A quink is the Welch rarebit face, the expression of one serving at tennis, or playing a difficult pool shot,— lifting the ball out of a bad golf hazard.

Women are quinked when they open a telegram; a boy, as he lights a fire-cracker. A girl, when in front of the glass, as she turns around to see if her underskirt is hanging down behind. A man, when he reads the ticker tape, during a panic, or is buttoning up the back of his wife's dress.

A waiter is quinked when his customer takes the change from the plate — how much will be the tip? The cook, when she is trying the candy in a cup of cold water. The mother, as she waits for the fever to turn. (See *Squinch.*)

A quink is that expression you have on your face just before the tooth is pulled; the minute before the flashlight goes off; when she pulls the trigger of the gun.

You are quinked when you wait for someone who is late, or when you hurry to catch the last train, with only four seconds to spare.

The fat man's face is quinked, when he tries to tie his own shoes. It is the face of the man, swimming under water, or of the playwright, on his opening night. (See *Snosh.*)

On Henry's face the lines were set,
  Distraught, he frowned and blinked;
Why? He was all alone, and yet
  He was severely quinked.

He heard the bell, but to the door
  He dared not go, to-day;
For he was quinked until that bore
  At last had walked away.

Quis'ty, *a.* Useful and reliable but not ornamental.

Quis'ter, *n.* A person or thing that is beloved
for its efficiency, character or worth, rather
than for decorative value.

She was not beautiful, but she was business-like; she knew
how to spell " its " and " it's " and " there " and " their "
and " they're." Her employer did not propose to her or take
her out to dinner, but he would not have parted with her for
a fortune. She was quisty. (See *Splooch.*)

The little tin motor-car your sporting friends call a " road-
louse " will go as far as his gas-drinking, tire-burning, oil-
consuming " Complex " and for one-tenth the money. It
isn't pretty, and it isn't expensive, but it's quisty.

Your jimmy-pipe is quisty, and so is that old mangy dress-
ing-gown and that comfortable, worn pair of corsets, and
those shabby shoes you hate to throw away. (See *Gefoojet.*)

Awful were the ugly apartments of the 80's, but the rooms
were large and airy; no such quisty flats nowadays.

Do you use an old-fashioned barber-style razor? Why?
Because it's quisty. That's why you use that prehistoric
stylographic pen, instead of a fountain, with a stiff,
scratchy nib. (See *Wijjicle.*)

Is your faithful, sympathetic wife a quister? Remember,
it's always the best-looking women who go through the divorce courts.

A pretty maid had Mrs. Slade,
And Mr. Slade admired her;
He used to glance at her askance
So much the Mrs. fired her.

A quisty maid now cooks for Slade,
She's uglier and thinner,
But Mrs. Slade is much dismayed;
Slade won't come home to dinner.

Quoob, *n.*   1. A misfit, an incompetent person.
  2. A person or thing obviously out of place.
  3. One not worldly wise.
Quoob, *v.*   To act differently than the rest; to
  commit a solecism; to be in the wrong place.

As you stand on the doorstep arrayed in your best, a sudden pang smites you. The door is opened. There is a look of blank astonishment, as you are ushered in. No hostess comes to greet you, no gay appareled guests are there. You are a quoob. The dinner is *next* Thursday, not to-night. (See *Zobzib.*)

Which is worse, to be the only one in evening dress, when all the rest are modestly clad, or to be yourself in street-clothes, surrounded by low-necks and jewelry? In either case, you are a quoob.

If you are a natural born quoob, you are the only one of all the audience to applaud, or cheer. At that sudden lull in the conversation, you are the one to speak aloud. " No, I must say, I prefer the old-fashioned night-gowns."

Sadly the quoob waits in the drug-store for the girl who never comes. (See *Quink.*) He goes to a party thought to be smart, to find he is the only one of importance.

A woman who is too tall is a quoob, or a man who is too short. So are you, when in rain coat and rubbers, after the sun has come out, or returning home in the morning, in your last night's dress suit.

> *I dreamed that I went out to walk*
>   *In but my night-shirt clad!*
> *I was a Quoob; I could not talk;*
>   *Oh, what a time I had!*
>
> *But that was nothing to my plight*
>   *When dining with Miss Lee —*
> *They all wore evening clothes that night*
>   *Except one Quoob —'twas me!*

QUOOB

Rawp, *n.* 1. A reliably-unreliable person.
2. One who means well. 3. A kind of husband.
Raw'pus, *a.* 1. Dilatory. 2. Semi-efficient.

The rawp can be absolutely depended upon to forget to
bring " that book " he borrowed and that now you need.
Unreliable? Oh, you can depend upon him never to keep
any engagement promptly; you would so much rather that
he would fail utterly — then you could properly scorn and
suppress him. (See *Zobzib.*)
But he *does* answer his letters — after a while. He *does*
mail letters — after they are sufficiently smooched and
crumpled in his coat pocket. The rawp, like the zobzib, is
almost always late for the train, late enough at any time to
give you a hygog.
Rawpus is the clerk who makes errors in his additions;
the typewriter who spells " to " in three ways — *all* wrong,
is also rawpus. (See *Splooch.*)
" Did you get me that spool of red silk I asked you to this
morning? " said Mrs. Smith. No, he forgot it. Mr. Smith
is a rawp.
" Did you ring up Green and tell him to send a man to
mow the lawn? " asked Mr. Smith. No, she didn't; Mrs.
Smith is a rawp.
And little Sammie Smith, who never goes to bed until he's
been told seven times — what then is he? A rawpet?

When Mr. Rawp arrived, the boat
Was sailing from the pier,
And Mrs. Rawp was there, afloat —
So far, and yet so near!

No wonder Mrs. Rawp was vexed,
For she returned, to find
He took the steamer sailing next,
And she was left behind!

Riz'gid-get, *n.* 1. A state of mental inertia or indecision; an inability to make up one's mind; a case of rival possibilities. 2. One who is lazily undecided.

You get the commonest, the most usual rizgidget in the restaurant: "What shall we have to eat?" But in seeking a gown, a hat or a wedding present, the rizgidget is always lying in wait for you, ready to infect you with mental sleeping sickness. It can catch you in the park and prevent your being able to decide even which side of the fountain to pass.

"Where shall we go on our vacation — to the mountains or the seashore?" This is the rizgidget which blooms perennially on June 1st. (See *Uglet.*)

"How much ought I to ask for it?" This is the rizgidget that has prevented many a sale.

"Which man shall I accept?" So the popular maiden is rizgidgeted.

"It looks like rain; shall we go or stay?" "Shall we sell our stocks, or hang on?" We cannot make up our minds; we are the victims of a rizgidget.

Why, every time you have a dinner party, you have the rizgidgets over whom to invite. (See *Cowcat.*)

> *A donkey with two bales of hay,*
> *So does the fable run,*
> *Rizgidgeted the livelong day,*
> *Deciding on "which one?"*
>
> *So, with a stupid brain that's stirred*
> *By sluggish fuss and fidget,*
> *Deciding what to name this word*
> *Do I delay — rizgidget!*

Rowtch, *n.* One who has elaborate gastronomic technique.

Rowtch, *v.* 1. To accomplish strange maneuvers over food by means of a knife and fork. 2. To eat audibly or with excessive unction.

For the " Kansas City " or " banjo grip," the rowtch, taking the fork in his left hand, places his thumb and little finger below, while the first, second and third fingers, as if touching the strings, press down upon the top of the instrument. (See *Wog.*)

The " Texan " grip is still more desperate; the fork is gripped as if about to stab — indeed it does stab, too!

Rowtching, however, can be done with a knife, as in the well known operation upon the tonsils, incidental to meals among our lower classes; the knife may be used to rowtch peas, or as a tool in that form of food-modeling which children affect.

More delicate and refined, more dainty and feminine is that form of rowtching which consists in jabbing a piece of meat upon the fork and adding dabs of potato, turnip and gravy until the utensil is heaped with its heterogeneous burden. Mashing and smoothing down of potato and smearing it with butter affords the rowtch opportunity for his plastic skill, or you may swirl your soda water glass.

Vegecide, the cutting of cooked potatoes and garden truck with a knife, is the only rowtch that obtains in high life.

A conscientious eater was
My mother's Uncle Bill;
We liked to see him eat, because
He liked to eat his fill.

And when he'd rowtched the meat and bread
And things all out of sight,
He pushed away his plate and said
" Lord, where's my appetite! "

81

Skinje, *v.* To feel shudderingly; to annoy
your fingers; to shrink from; to set your teeth
on edge.

Skinjed, *p.p.* To have one's tactile nerves
outraged.

Skin'jid, *a.* Harsh, rough or gritty.

Did you ever skinje a broken finger-nail on satin? "Alias,
Jimmy Valentine" can rub his finger-tips on sandpaper, but
it's too skinjid for poor little Me.

My Aunt Eliza's hands are skinjid; no wonder, she *will*
wash them in soft-soap. And every time I kiss her chapped
lips, I am horribly skinjed. (See *Vorge.*)

James Whitcomb Riley, in a pathetic little verse, tells of
a sensitive, delicate young lady who loved to draw her fin-
ger-nails in long, sweet scratches down the plastered walls,
skinjing them pathetically. You and I prefer to scratch
bricks or blackboards — they are more skinjid. Do new
towels skinje you? Do you skinje at wet velvet? Can you
bite a skinjid file? Your collar — has it a skinjid edge?

"Put more starch in them lace curtains before you iron
'em," says Mrs. O'Hatchet to the hired girl. "Mr. Mas-
ters always likes to feel of 'em before he goes to bed." (See
Kripsle.)

> *As skinjid as a plaster wall,*
> *As skinjid as a file,*
> *So is the world when I am broke;*
> *I cannot laugh or smile.*
>
> *But when my purse is full and fat*
> *I know no teasing twinge;*
> *I meet so much to giggle at*
> *Nothing can make me skinje!*

Sky'scrim-ble, *v.*   1. To go off at a tangent;
to fly into space.   2. To make a wild flight
from an untenable intellectual position.

The acrobat on the flying trapeze skyscrimbles in a thrilling arc from perch to perch. So skyscrimbles the philosopher into words of seven syllables, when you ask him about the Deity. (See *Gubble* and *Edicle.*)

A woman caught in an inconsistency skyscrimbles through an hour of fantastic argument.

When Wilson won, red Republicans skyscrimbled up into the Democratic fold. (See *Eegot.*)

Tell a Socialist that "You can't change human nature," — he skyscrimbles in Marxian metaphysics.

So, when you complain of your laundry, or your telephone service, or the railroad company's neglect, men skyscrimble, passing the blame from one to another.

Ask one actress about another's age. . . . "Why, she was in the Murray Hill Stock Company when Dustin Farnum used to " . . . etc., etc., etc. . . . A skyscrimble.

> *I asked a Suffragette one day,*
>   *Whose wits were neat and nimble,*
> *Why she had rouged her cheeks that way —*
>   *She did a quick skyscrimble.*

> *I told a man 'twas funny that*
>   *His overcoat was new*
> *While wifey wore her last year's hat —*
>   *And he skyscrimbled, too!*

Slub, *n.* 1. A mild illness, that does not really incapacitate. 2. A "headache." 3. An indisposition, manufactured for an especial occasion.

Slub'by, *a.* Feeling the necessity of a good excuse.

A slub is a cold, a headache, a boil or any affection in the disreputable underworld of disease. There's nothing of the aristocracy of pain in the slub. It is, so to speak, a mere working illness.

Men's slubs, however, are more intense than women's. A man when he has a slub, says, "Oh pshaw! it's nothing." But he expects, all the same, to be assiduously attended. Every woman in the household must minister to his misery. (See *Varm.*)

Women have slubs innumerable, and for the most part say nothing about them, unless they want an excuse for staying away from a party. When the society woman has a slub, she sends for a good looking doctor. (See *Alibosh.*)

Children, however, are oftener slubby — when they don't want to go to school or to church the slub works overtime. (See *Uglet* and *Moosoo.*)

Shop-girls are not allowed to have slubs.

> " I have a slub! " the maiden said,
>   " I cannot go with you.
> " You'll have to go without me, Fred! "
>   And Fred felt slubby, too.
>
> But when, at ten o'clock, or so,
>   He found his girl disdainful
> Maxixing with his hated foe
>   Fred's slub grew really painful!

Snosh, *n.* 1. Vain talk; 1000 words to the square idea. 2. A talker from whom no results are expected; one who cannot be taken seriously. 3. A project or enterprise that is born dead.

Wall Street is where the snosh abounds. Advertise, circularize, collect and disappear — that's how they work the gold-mine snosh. (See *Alibosh.*)

Queer, isn't it — a man who's always " full of schemes " is always a snosh, while a crank with one idea may succeed. Why? A snosh is always imitating something. He is the theatrical manager who follows up a successful play with a third-rate duplicate.

But, talking about plays, did you ever talk to a society woman who was writing one? It's a snosh. In the first place, she won't finish it until the year 1977 and then it will take her a double-lifetime to find a big enough fool to produce it. Broadway is lined with snoshes — but the word isn't necessarily theatrical. The smart restaurant that insists on evening dress is a snosh — and so is an actress who says she loves you.

In Reno dwells the married snosh. Any wedding performed upon a bride and groom under the age of 25 is a snosh. So is a marriage with a Count. (See *Pawdle.*)

Miss Pittsburgh swore that she would wed
A title, and by Gosh,
Miss Pittsburgh did; her father paid
A million for a snosh.

And now, although he swears at her,
It is a Count that swears,
And over eyes he's black-and-blued
A coronet she wears!

Spigg, *n.* 1. Any decoration of overt vanity.
2. Extrinsic charms. 3. Things worn obviously to attract notice.
Spig'get-y, *a.* Prinked, elaborately adorned.

Paint, powder, dyed hair, court plaster patches, artificial dimples, highly manicured and rouged nails, blacking under the eyes, whiting under the chin, rouged ears, lead-penciled eyebrows, loaded eye-lashes are spigg. (See *Wowze.*)

Jewelry is spigg; spigg is the treasure-chest of would-be beauty, the ammunition of the bogus Cupid.

In some latitudes, ladies are spigged with tattoo marks and nose-rings; in others, with marceled hair and low-necked gowns. (See *Varm.*)

Men spigg themselves with fancy socks and curled moustaches. In the cart-horse parade, Old Dobbin spiggs his braided tail with ribbons.

For spigg is nothing but a vanity that is not ashamed to advertise itself; but advertising is one of the most difficult of arts, wherefore now its appeal is as grotesque as the three fat seasick plumes in the dowager's hair, and now it is as delicate as the violets in a debutante's bosom.

> So spiggety was cousin Grace,
>   When I was there last night,
> I could not even see her face;
>   She was a shocking sight!
>
> " Why all this flour and whitewash, dear?
>   Why so much black-and-red? "
> " Because I'd feel so nude, this year,
>   Without my spigg," she said.

Spil'lix, *n.* 1. Undeserved good luck; acci-
dental success. 2. A lucky stroke, beyond
one's normal ability.

Spil'lix-y, *a.* Exceptional, lucky, uncharac-
teristic. Untrue to " form."

At pool, tennis or golf, the spillix aids the amateur with
proverbial luck. A spillix is winning a prize in the lottery;
is the business deal, that unexpectedly goes through; is meeting an influential friend when you are in your best clothes.
Getting a position by inadvertently happening to be right on
the spot.

A bargain is a spillix; an exciting conversation overheard
on the telephone. (See *Frowk.*)

Thousands of people, intending to cross on the Titanic,
took the next boat following — and boasted of the spillix.

It's a spillix, to find money in the street; also to discover
that the chaperon is more charming than the girl herself.
Through a spillix, you blunder into success. (See *Zobzib.*)

Every young May that weds a rich old December, prays
for a spillix, but he seldom dies to leave her a fascinating
widow in becoming robes of black.

A spillix is a lucid interval, or the bright remark of a fool.

His first shot to the bull's eye flew —
He would not shoot — for then
It was a spillix, and he knew
He would not score again.

So, when he wed the girl he sought,
We thought 'twas rather funny —
It was a spillix; for she thought,
Alas, that he had money!

Splooch, *n.*　1. A failure, a ruin.　2. One who doesn't know his business; a bad amateur. 3. Exorbitantly overpaid service.

One thinks at first naturally of a restaurant; there are more splooch waiters than anything else in the world.　Next, come servant girls, the splooch that burns the soup and leaves the salt out of the bread.　A cake with an ingrowing stomach is a splooch.　A suit of clothes that looks anxious about the shoulderblades — wet hay — bug-eaten potato plants and pears with worms inside — splooches all.

Most musical comedies are splooches, most stories in the magazines, most janitors.　(See *Jurp.*)

What then, of the dentist who pulls out the sound tooth by mistake, or the surgeon who takes out your appendix but leaves his eye-glasses inside?　He's a medico-splooch.

Then there's the vaudeville juggler who splooches the balls and the singer who's off the key.　(See *Snosh.*)

Every day on Wall Street ten thousand lambs make splooch investments, hoping to become captains of finance.

> *I'll never dine at Mack's again;*
> *The splooch that slings the eats*
> *He makes me wait an hour, and then*
> *He serves me corn, for beets!*
>
> *Last night I ordered Irish stew,*
> *And there my wife's old brooch*
> *That she had lost a year or two*
> *Was hidden in the splooch!*

SPLOOCH

Spuzz, *n.* 1. Mental energy, an aggressive intellect. 2. Stamina, force, spice.
Spuz′zard, *n.* An active, forceful thinker. 2. A cocktail with a " kick " in it.
Spuz′zy, *a.* 1. Highly seasoned. Charged with brain-electricity.

Theodore Roosevelt and Kaiser Wilhelm have spuzz. Demiourgos, maker of men, gave them an extra dash of the tabasco. (See *Persotude.*)

Spuzz in acting, in writing, or in business is what brings in the money.

Spuzz welcomes competition; it is always ready for the fray.

You can't down the spuzzard; he is elastic, and bounces up after every failure.

The spuzzard is the girl who could " just die dancing." She answers her letters the day they are received.

The farmer with no spuzz to him can never lift the mortgage; but the spuzzy intensive Italian down the road is educating his sons to be doctors and lawyers.

Spuzz is that getaheadative zip, tang, and racehorse enthusiasm that has for its motto, " Do it now."

A good Welch rarebit has spuzz; so has a dry Martini — but it's the wrong kind. (See *Looblum.*)

> *How I admire a Suffragette!*
> *No matter what she does,*
> *She has red corpuscles, you bet!*
> *She has a lot of spuzz!*
>
> *And yet — I would not marry her;*
> *But some shy, timid elf,*
> *Some clinging flower shall be my bride;*
> *I'll find the spuzz, myself!*

Squinch, *n.* A nervous, anxious state of mind; a palpitating desire to succeed beyond one's deserts.

Squinch, *v.* To watch and wait, hoping things will turn one's own way; to anticipate.

No squinch like the sailor's, sniffing the weather from the catheads, or wherever he sniffs it from — unless it is the farmer, squinching for sun or rain that will bring a harvest of crops enough to pay the interest on the mortgage.

You squinch the stock market for a rise or fall; but no matter how you squinch U. S. Steel Common, there's always someone squinching it the other way.

Then there's the lottery squinch — or there used to be, wondering if the winning number will end in 6.

The candidate is on the squinch before election with his ear to the ground. President Wilson squinches Mexico as anxiously as a village girl squinches her beau for a proposal. (See *Quink.*)

See the House Manager of a theatre in the box office squinching the crowd coming in for the evening performance! So I squinch this word, hoping that it will become popular.

Behind his geography, little Willie squinches his teacher, as he reads, "The White Slaver's Revenge," or, "Saved by Eugenics." (See *Kipe.*)

> *I knew that I was squinched, because*
> *When e'er I spoke of rings,*
> *Or wedding bells, or marriage laws,*
> *She looked unuttered things.*
>
> *But still I flirted, standing pat,*
> *And did not yield an inch;*
> *I told her I was married — that*
> *Was how I fooled her squinch!*

TASHIVATE

Tash-i-va'tion, *n.* The art of replying by means of reciprocal tones.

Tash'i-vate, *v.* To reply without attention; to speak aimlessly, or without interest, as to a child.

Tash'i-vat-ed, *p.p.* Absorbed in more interesting things; inattentive; answered perfunctorily.

Have you acquired the art of tashivation? Can you read the newspaper right along through your wife's gossip, or your little daughter's prattle? This is the secret of true domesticity; it is the science of being a husband.

The actress has an ear trained to distinguish emotions, and a tongue trained to answer them without the conscious use of her brain. A friend tells her a long, dull story, and her mind wanders through the Elysian Fields of her own experiences, unheeding. Suddenly the tale ends — "And there she was, right in the room with him!" What was it all about? Never mind, the answer is easy: "Well, *what* do you think of that?" (See *Drillig.*)

Tashivation is answering without listening, as one speaks to a beggar — as one talks at a crowded reception, as one answers the man who asks for a loan.

When a man explains machinery to a woman, she tashivates, her mind on pleasanter things; and so, when a woman explains fashions to a man. (See *Varm.*)

> *Why do I tashivate, and say*
> *"Oh, yes," and "Really?"—"Yes?"*
> *Because although she talks, I try*
> *To read my book, I guess.*
>
> *I nod and smile, and speak, sedate;*
> *My wife keeps on her chatter.*
> *So long as I can tashivate*
> *Her questions do not matter.*

Thusk, *n.* 1. Something that has quickly passed away. 2. A precocious memory; an unnatural feeling of remoteness.

Thusk'y, *a.* So near, and yet so far.

Thusky are the sounds in the street, as you lie ill in bed in summer. Thusky are your old love letters, tied in blue ribbons, the last one postmarked fully a week ago. (See *Iobink*.)

Yesterday's newspaper is thusky, and last year's popular song. Thusky are the novels that six months since were talked about and read. Thusky are last winter's styles. (See *Gowyop*.)

While you are abroad, the American newspapers are thusky; when you are returning, all Europe is a thusk.

Thusky is the house you once lived in; your old sweetheart of college days.

Which is the thuskiest,— a dead actor, an ex-president, or a popular hero, now laid on the shelf?

> *I met a thusk the other day;*
> *Three times I had to look*
> *Before I recognized him — say,*
> *'Twas only Doctor Cook!*

> *How thusky, now, his polar jest!*
> *As thusky as the way*
> *A joke would sound, if 'twere expressed*
> *In slang of yesterday!*

Tin′tid-dle, *n.*   1. An imaginary conversation.
2. A witty retort, thought of too late, a mental postscript.

Tin-tid-di-la′tion, *n.* Optimistic day-dreaming.

Oh, the bright reply you thought of, after you had gone — the crushing answer that you *might* have given! Who does not know the tardy tintiddle? The questions you forgot to ask, the terms you forgot to make, the repairs you did not ask. *Was* there any closet in that corner room? Now, *did* that include water, or not? Tintiddling comes with tantalizing thought. (See *Iobink.*)

When you rehearsed your speech the night before, the chorus of applause came tintiddling to your ears. And when tintiddling you proposed to the girl, she fell gratefully into your arms.

When in tintiddilation, you applied for that position, how noble was your pose — how convincing were your words! But they were only tintiddles, and tintiddles never come out as you expect. (See *Bimp.*)

Chastely tintiddling are the wedding anticipations of the bride! (See *Jujasm.*)

> *Tintiddling vainly, I proposed*
> *To Kate — and was accepted.*
> *Next day (as you might have supposed),*
> *I was with scorn rejected.*

> *How oft, tintiddling all alone,*
> *I'm witty, wise, defiant —*
> *But in real life, no one has known*
> *That I'm a mental giant!*

Ud'ney, *n.* 1. A beloved bore; one who loves you but does not understand you; a fond, but stupid relative. 2. An old friend whom you have outgrown.

Your mother, your doting aunt, your dull, but affectionate husband, your favorite brother's wife; or the man your sister is engaged to — udneys all. You hate to hurt their feelings; would they not do anything in the world for you? You go to them in your troubles and you forget them in your pleasures. You hate to write to them, but manage to scrawl hasty and vapid notes. (See *Uglet.*)

The udney gives you gifts of clothing you can't possibly wear, and expects you to rave over them.

Or, the udney is someone who likes you more than you like him. He is like an affectionate dog, always under foot or licking your hand.

In the pathetic slavery that women endure, not the slavery of women to men — but that of women to women — the udney has the master hand. The blindly doting parent, whose daughter "has no secrets from her," rules with a rod of sugar. Though her daughter may be old enough to have to "touch up" her hair — yet so long as she has a "Miss" before her name will it be her doom to be the willing slave and pet of an unconscious udney. (See *Varm.*)

> *Jane's mother nothing did forbid;*
> *She was an udney, though —*
> *Because, whatever Janey did*
> *Her mother had to know.*

> *"Of course he'll marry you," one day,*
> *She said to guilty Jane,*
> *"Or else why should he kiss you, pray?"*
> *How could the girl explain!*

Ug'let, *n.* 1. An unpleasant duty. 2. Something one puts off too long.
Ug'gle, *v.* 1. To procrastinate respecting the inevitable. 2. To do something one dislikes.

Having to have your teeth filled is an uglet; you wait and wait, trying to find the time — and the courage.

Getting up early in the morning is an uglet; inquiring regularly about convalescents; and getting a spring hat, or a new fall suit — delaying until you are the last one in town. (See *Vorge.*)

It's an uglet to clean your top bureau drawer; and calling on the Wilsons — darning your stockings — or buying a wedding present, or having your picture taken. (See *Digmix.*)

"Oh, I've simply *got* to do that!" But — how long you delay in inviting the Ransoms to dinner! It's an uglet.

Paying the doctor's bill is the universal uglet. (See *Igmoil.*) But answering letters from people you haven't seen for a long time is worse.

> *It was an uglet that I feared;*
> *It grew, and grew, and grew,*
> *And long I had to dree my weird —*
> *That deed I dared not do;*
>
> *And yet it must be done! In fear,*
> *Unto my wife, I said:*
> *" Your hat is NOT becoming, dear —*
> *You never should wear red!"*

Unk, *n.* 1. An unwelcome present, an inappropriate, undesirable or distasteful gift. 2. A duplicate wedding present. 3. A souvenir, or picture postcard.

These are the classic unks that women give to men — unwearable neckties, hand-embroidered suspenders, smokeless cigars —" La Flor de Chinatown!" They give them sleeve-button unks, unks made of shiny black leather. "It's *so* hard to find gifts for a man!" (See *Gefoojet.*)

Men give in return, feminine unks — flowers that don't match a girl's gown; perfumery in fancy bottles; a dozen pairs of gloves of an off color; souvenir jewelry boxes with pictures of the State Capitol on top; impossible paper cutters; ivory handled nail files elaborately carved, that will not file. (See *Quisty* and *Diabob.*)

Women of uncertain age receive unks in the form of bed-shoes, with an old-maid implication; linen collars, with stiff tabby-cat bows in front, disgustingly neat —" so nice for business!" There they are, in back of the bureau drawer, yellowing with age.

When you were married, you received thirty-four wedding unks; nine pie knives and forty-five pickle forks.

A gold pencil that won't write is an unk; so is that padded seal volume of Tennyson on the shelf beneath the center table. (See *Gorgule.*)

What is an unk? That thing that lies
  Upon your bureau, there!
You have outlived your first surprise;
  You do not even care.

Its faint and foolish life is done,
  It is a mere negation; —
An unused souvenir of one
  Without imagination!

Varm, *n.* 1. The quintessence of sex. 2. One who is characteristically womanish or man-like.

Var′mic, *a.* Monosexually psychologic. 2. Provoking intersexual antipathy.

A man in love thinks himself attracted to a woman because she is feminine, and different from him; in reality, it is because he thinks she is different from other women. He does not discover her varm. Other girls are vain, tricky, deceitful and illogical — *she* is a creature unique.

But, when he is married, she becomes unexpectedly varmic. He watches her egoistic poses before the mirror, and the first time their " togetherness " is broken by her confidential delights with another woman, he sees her varm.

To a man, there is something he hates in woman, if not in women. It's the subtle antipathy of sex — the things women tell each other — the things they *do* — it's the varm.

But so women secretly hate men — hate their childishness, their superiority, their insanity and their blindness.

" Just like a woman! " So do men voice their varm.

Your wife's bureau drawers are varmic. So is a tea-room, or a woman's club, or a co-educational college, or the ladies' dressing room of a fashionable restaurant. (See *Spigg.*)

Smoking tobacco is no longer varmic. (See *Ovotch.*)

How would you like to see your husband at a prize fight? There varm is violent.

> *I hate a girl — but my Hortense*
> *Is not the average woman;*
> *She has more brains, she has more sense —*
> *In fact, she's almost human.*
>
> *Or, so I thought, until, one day,*
> *She lost that previous charm,*
> *I overheard her talk with May —*
> *Hortense was but a varm!*

101

Vilp, *n.*   1. A bad loser, an unsportsmanlike
   player.   2. A gloating victor, or one who is
   intoxicated by success.

Vil'pous, *a.*   Unscrupulous, cheating in games.

The vilp is always explaining why he lost the game and
usually blaming the fault upon someone else — he " usually
plays a much better game " than the one you see.   This time,
it is only because he has the rheumatism, or didn't get any
sleep last night.   (See *Slub.*)

The vilp plays to win — plays for the stakes or the prize.
Women vilps have even been known to cheat at cards to gain
a half-pound box of candy tied with yellow ribbon.

The vilp takes advantage of all his opponent's slips, calls
all fouls, but does not notice his own.   He crows over his
victim when he wins, and sulks when he loses.   He bullies
his opponent, and whines when he comes out last.   (See
Igmoil.)

There is no sex to the vilp; the women at the bridge and
the men at the poker table are alike vilpous.   (See *Gorm.*)

There is no sport like Love, and he
Or she who plays the game
Must play to win; and so, maybe,
The vilp is not to blame.

" All's fair in love and war," they say,
So women cheat and fight,
And men compete the vilpous way.
But does that make it right?

Voip, *n.*   Food that gives no gastronomic pleas-
ure; any provender that is filling, but taste-
less.
Voip, *v.*   To eat hurriedly, without tasting.

Every morning, millions of Americans go forth sustained
for work, but cheated out of the pleasures of a real repast —
they have merely fed on voip.
Pop corn was the original voip, discovered by the Pilgrim
Fathers. Next came crackers, ham-sandwiches-without-but-
ter and the sawdusty provender of railroad lunch counters.
(See *Mooble.*)
Ginger snaps are voip; so are buns and doughnuts. Lastly
came the reign of glorified voip in decorated pasteboard packages — breakfast foods of all degrees from birdseed up to
dried peas.
New York has discovered the art of transforming any food
into voip, by the simple expedient of making you eat it standing.   (See *Uglet.*)

> At breakfast, when on voip I feed,
>   Mechanically chewing,
> My listless palate does not heed,
>   Or know what it is doing.
>
> I oft forget, when I am through,
>   And wonder if I've fed!
> I have to feel my stomach to
>   Be sure I've breakfasted!

Vorge, *n.*   1. Voluntary suffering; unnecessary agony.   2. The lure of the uncertain.

Vor'gid, *a.*   Morbidly fascinating; interested in horrors.

Peary was a vorgid man; twenty years of freezing half to death did not conquer his appetite. When he had found the North Pole, he didn't know what to do with it. To him, life was just one vorge after another, pulling sledges, eating shoes and candles, sleeping in a bearskin bag. (See *Yab.*)

Whence comes the vogue of the vorge? As a child, you could not help putting your tongue to frozen iron, although you knew the skin would stick to it; the deed was vorgid. You put beans up your nose, and wheat up your stocking. You tattooed your arms; and that attractive sore compelled your touch. Vorgid was castor oil, and bitter medicines. All these things were horrid, but you did them and boasted of the vorge. It is vorgid to pull out your own tooth.

But how about him who escorts his homely cousin to a dance, and gets her partners? Is this less vorgid?

Oh, very vorgid is he who makes a speech, but vorgider far the groom at a fashionable wedding.

Are you vorgid? Do you enjoy doing palestric exercises in the Gym, or a cold bath on winter mornings? (See *Gloogo.*) Do you look forward, vorgidly, to the happy Xmastide?

Vorgid is women's talk about their " operations."

> *Oh, vorgid 'tis to pant and strain*
> *And tug, the athlete thinks;*
> *And it is vorgid, in the rain,*
> *To golf o'er soggy links.*
>
> *But it is vorgider, by far,*
> *Than such palestric feat,*
> *To give that lady in the car*
> *Your Oh-so-longed-for seat!*

Vo'ri-an-der, *n.* 1. A woman who chases after men, instead of being chased. 2. A woman who telephones to men, or invites herself to dinners at his expense.

Vo'ri-an-der, *v.* 1. To act as above described; to inflict oneself upon an unwilling entertainer. Women's overt competition for men.

To most men the voriander is anathema. He would prefer to ask the dullest girl in the world to dinner than to entertain the prettiest, who has invited herself.

Sly and patent are the tricks of the voriander. She may telephone you: " Have you got your car out of storage yet? " Or she may say, point-blank: " Say, isn't there a dinner coming to me along about now? " (See *Eegot.*)

The voriander is sometimes pretty, but never attractive. Her attempts are usually dodged, but she still persists. " Confound it, I just *will* get that man! " she says, and proceeds to voriander.

Never introduce a friend to a voriander. There are other kinder ways of getting rid of her. A cat can be kissed to death, or smothered in fresh butter; not the voriander. You have simply to leave town.

The voriander is " crazy " over you, and your purse. She writes you perfumed notes, she telephones you during business hours. (See *Drillig.*)

Many vorianders are over thirty years of age.

Beware the voriander, boy,
With mouth that kisses and torments.
She only loves you to enjoy
Expensive foods at your expense.

Beware the voriander, let
Her scented notes unanswered be;
She's after just what she can get;
And when you're broke, she'll let you be!

105

Whin′kle, *n.*   1. Graciousness, with ulterior in-
tent; a hypocritical politeness.   2. A glow of
vanity.
Whin′kle, *v.*   To appear over-cordial or sus-
piciously amiable; to act snobbishly.

Some beam with a merely personal vanity; they whinkle
from sheer self-satisfaction.   But when Jones saw me, he
whinkled till I thought his front teeth would spill out of his
face.   Why?   I was talking to a millionaire.   (See *Eegot.*)

So the match-making Mamma whinkles at that desirable
young man, who is calling upon Bessie.

So the book-agent whinkles as he shows you his samples;
and the insurance agent, just before you kick him out.

Whinkles the floor-walker, like the girls at a seashore resort,
beckoning the only nice young man; but the floor-walker
whinkles not when you return a " thirty-six " waist for a
" thirty-eight."   (See *Jurp.*)

The mother whinkles when you praise the baby, and the
proud undertaker when he first displays the corpse.

Mark the whinkling landlady, showing the third floor front
to the prospective lodger.   " You'll find it a very comfortable
home here; everyone has always been happy here — very!
Nice and sunny . . . plenty of towels . . . closet . . . nice,
soft bed — no bugs in *my* house.   Lovely bureau, plenty of
room for all your things.   I am *sure* you couldn't do better."

How whinkles the pallid clerk at his employer's jokes.

> *When first my motor-car I bought,*
> *The salesman wagged his tail —*
> *He whinkled till I almost thought*
> *He'd kiss me, for the sale.*

> *But when the poppet-valves were strained,*
> *And had to be repaired —*
> *No whinkling then, when I complained;—*
> *The salesman merely glared!*

Wij′ji-cle, *n.* A perverse or contradictory article of furniture; any household contrivance that is always out of order.

"You'll find no wijjicles in *this* house," said the agent as he unlocked the front door. "It's in perfect order." And yet, before I had left I had found:

Eight window-screens that wouldn't go up or down; loose boards in the dining-room and three on the stairs that squeaked; a leak in the roof, a smoky fireplace, three cupboard doors that wouldn't shut, four closet doors that would swing open, and a long, phlegmatic bath-tub that it took three-quarters of an hour to fill, through its reluctant faucet. (See *Quisty.*)

But I must confess I brought in my own wijjicles, too. Reader, you know them well —

The folding camp-chairs that can't be unfolded, the three-legged tables that tip over, the rocking-chairs that bite you on the shins in the dark and patent spring-rockers that squeak; the unoiled door, the mirrors with wavy glass, the bureau drawers that stick and the step-ladders that won't stay open; the baby-carriages that are always in the way; plush furniture that sticks, and painted chairs that come off on your back; screen doors that bang, and rugs on slippery floors, the table that balances unsteadily.

But the worst of all, is the pencil with its lead broken far up inside the wood. (See *Moosoo.*)

> *I bought a rubber fountain pen;*
> *"Non-leakable," the clerk*
> *Assured me confidently, when*
> *He showed me how 'twould work.*

> *But now that wijjicle and I*
> *Into the bath-tub go*
> *When I must write my letters. Why?*
> *Well, things are safer, so!*

Wog, *n.*   An attached foreign body, an unorna-
ment.

Wog, *v.*   To daub fantastically; to decorate an
unconscious victim.

Wogged, *p.p.*   To have any intrinsic defect or visible superfluity.

Wog'gy, *a.*   Unpleasantly adorned.

Have you ever seen the gentleman with the Niagara-Falls
moustache? Pretty woggy, what? When beautiful Bessie
drinks buttermilk and forgets her napkin, what can you say?
Such things must not be told.   Think of Bessie — with a wog!
You must turn away your head and blush — or else Bessie
must.   Wogs embarrass.   (See *Pooje.*)

But facial stalactites are not the only wogs, alas! Milli-
cent's hair is wogged — prithee catch the hairpin before it
falls.   As you pick a thread that wogs your wife's grey
gown, she discovers a blonde hair on your coat-collar, the
most embarrassing of all wogs.

Pittsburgh wogs its women with spots of smut, black as
court-plaster patches.   You really ought to get a new dress
suit, for yours is seven years old and wildly wogged with
grease-spots — where you spilled the pink-and-green ice cream
into your lap and where the Swedish waiter bathed your
shoulders with cauliflower soup.   There is a wog of ragged
braid on the bottom of your torn skirt, a running wog in
your silk stocking.   (See *Splooch.*)

Don't get wogged!   (See *Zobzib.*)

> *I never care for onion soup —*
> *For onion soup, and hash,*
> *And scrambled eggs remind me of*
> *My uncle's red moustache;*
>
> *For that was what we had to eat*
> *When Uncle Silas, togged*
> *In Sunday raiment, came to dine,*
> *And got his whiskers wogged!*

WOG

Wowze, *n.* 1. A woman who is making a fool of herself and doesn't know it. 2. Any ridiculous and undignified object. 3. A spectacular exhibition of unconscious humor.

Wowze, *v.* To act with a misguided belief in one's charm; to cavort hopelessly.

Have you ever seen a painfully conscientious amateur tangoist counting her steps? " One-two-three — *hold!* " She's a wowze! Have you ever been to church on Easter Sunday in the country? There are wowzes galore.

An elderly maiden being kittenish — a perfect wowze! An elderly aunt, talking baby-talk to her infant niece — the wowze pathetic. A female art-student — the wowze æsthetic.

A wowze is a female poem-reciter in a hot parlor; a fat woman in swimming; an overgrown girl in short skirts; an angry landlady; a miss in curl-papers. A shirt waist of plaid silk is a wowze, and a cook, learning to skate. (See *Frowk.*)

A literary lady, trying to look " artistic " — she's a wowze and her gown is wowzier.

The wowze-social: — A woman who doesn't like it, trying to smoke. (See *Ovotch.*)

> *Miss Henderson was meek and mild,*
> *But, through her black silk veil,*
> *She drank a glass or two of milk —*
> *(She had been drinking ale.)*

> *Then, answering our wild applause,*
> *She rose with smiles and bows.*
> *She'd proved that she was clever, but*
> *She was a perfect wowse!*

Wox, *n.*   A state of placid enjoyment; sluggish
satisfaction.
Wox'y, *a.*   Contented; ruminant; at peace with
the world.

As the glutted anaconda, after swallowing a sheep alive,
rests for a benign month or two underenath the tum-tum tree,
thinking of home and mother, while the gross lump in his
stomach gradually declines and lessens — so is the wox of
the woman well and appropriately gowned, especially if that
dress of hers has been successfully made over beyond all recog-
nition.

Woxy is the broker, as stocks go up.   Woxy is the fisher-
man, when the fish begin to bite.   Woxy is the legatee, when
the lawsuit is over and his inheritance is paid.

After your long tramp in the rain, after your bath and hot
dinner, you sit by the open fire in a wox.

There is no joy but calm, say the Buddhists; it's better to
be woxy than excited with rapture.   (See *Jujasm.*)

The author is in a wox; his story has been accepted.   Woxy
is the actor in a good hotel at last, after three weeks of one-
night stands; when he pushes the bell, something delightful
is sure to happen.   There can be no wox, alas, without a
previous annoyance.   (See *Fud.*)   But is not all the maddening bustle and trouble of moving worth — when you are
finally settled and at ease, with every carpet down and every
picture hung — the homelike, comfortable wox that follows?

> *I ploughed my way through wind and storm*
> *   To call on Fanny White;*
> *And in her parlor I was warm*
> *   And woxy with delight.*

> *'Twas not because I loved her though —*
> *   For I was fairly foxy;*
> *I'd sold her Life Insurance, so*
> *   That's why I felt so woxy!*

Wum'gush, *n.* 1. An insincere affectation of cordiality; hypocritical compliments. 2. Women's flattery of women; pretended friendship. 3. A feminine fib.

Do women criticise each other to their faces? Do they find fault with their chocolates, their looks, their clothes, their jests? No, not until the front door is closed; till then, they slobber wumgush. (See *Varm.*)

And yet, if one man offers another a cigarette, the tobacco may be called "rotten!" without peril or anger.

Men have small use for wumgush; their compliments are profane ridicule and simulated enmity.

A man calls his best friend a "damned fool"; a woman calls her worst enemy, "My dear!" (See *Alibosh.*)

How women must fear each other! They smooth their rival's hair; lovingly, they readjust her jabot and pat her hands lingeringly.

"How well you're looking, my dear!". . . and yards and yards of wumgush.

"Oh, I've had such a wonderful time! How charming of you to have asked me. Now, you *must* come to see us."— Wumgush. (See *Gubble.*)

Wumgush is the frothy foam of society chatter.

Wumgush is the sunshine through which fly the wasps of sarcasm. (See *Flooijab.*)

> *The wumgush Clara spills on Lou,*
> *Whene'er they meet, and kiss,*
> *Would seem to prove a friendship true,*
> *But it amounts to this,—*

> *" Your waist is soiled; and, oh, that hat!*
> *Trimmed it yourself, I know!*
> *You never ought to grin like that,*
> *It makes your crow's feet show!"*

Xen'o-gore, *n.*   1. An interloper; one who is
de trop, or keeps you from things or persons
of greater interest.   2. A self-invited guest,
who stays too long.

The xenogore is a person who doesn't belong, but doesn't
know it.   It is the shopper who paws over goods, and prevents customers from buying; an extra woman, who drops in
when you want to play whist; or the creature who appears at
dinner-time, when you have just enough for the family and
no more; who invites himself into your motor-car, crowding
you miserably.   He annoys you when you are talking business, and spoils the sale.

Children in the room, when you are calling, are xenogores.
(See *Kidloid.*)

Someone talking to you, when you want to listen to that
interesting conversation opposite, is a xenogore.

A xenogore is likely to be anyone of your wife's relations
or friends; but it's sure to be that girl you have to escort
home, and don't want to.   (See *Uglet.*)

A girl who accompanies a couple in love is a xenogore.   (See
Vorge.)

> *I longed to see her Paris gowns,*
> *And hear about my aunts,*
> *And all those queer cathedral towns —*
> *She'd just returned from France.*

> *I'd scarcely welcomed her — before*
> *I'd told her she was thinner,*
> *There came a ring — a xenogore!*
> *Of course he stayed to dinner.*

Yab, *n.* 1. A monomaniac or fanatic, interested in one thing. 2. A favorite topic of
discussion, or conversation.
Yab'by, *a.* Talking continually on a single
topic.
Yabs, *a.* Foolishly interested or absorbed.

People used to be yabs on religion, but you seldom see a
gospel yab, now that Dowie has passed from sight.   Still,
there's a pretty pronounced Christian Science yab on in ideal-
istic circles.   Business yabs, yes; but your wife won't stand
for it at the supper-table, unless your guest is a good, heavy
buyer.   (See *Eegot.*)
The musician lives in a yab-world of his own.   He doesn't
understand ordinary English.
Some men are yabs over women, some have a horrible baseball yab that will last over way into February; but the worst
of all is a yabby actor, telling you how good he is.   (See
Leolump.)
Polonius, had he lived, would have said to Hamlet, " Still
yabs about my daughter! "
The White Slave yab is almost over and the Sex yab is mute
in the magazines; the Bigyab is Tango with a capital Q.
The egoist is yabs about himself; the Englishman is yabby
over sport, the Hebrew over money.   Me, my yab is " Burgess Unabridged."   (See *Gloogo.*)

> *Once a little girl in Phœnix*
> *Arizona wrote to me;*
> *She was yabs about eugenics,*
> *And was healthy as a flea.*

> *But although my Jane was poorly,*
> *And was half the time in bed,*
> *I was yabs about her, surely,*
> *So I married her, instead.*

Yam′noy, *n.* 1. A bulky, unmanageable object; an unwieldy or slippery parcel. 2. Something you don't know how to carry.
Yam′noy, *v.* 1. To inflict with much luggage. 2. To carry many parcels at once.

Did you ever see a woman trying to move a Morris chair — or carry a rocker through a screen door? (See *Wijjicle*.) She is struggling with a yamnoy. She can carry a baby with ease and skill, but it's a yamnoy to a bachelor.

The yamnoy is a sheet of window glass carried on a windy day; a dripping umbrella that you don't know where to place; a bird-cage or a bowl of fish, that you don't dare trust in the moving van. (See *Uglet*.)

To yamnoy is to move a ladder or place it upright, or to carry a lawn mower home from the city.

> *A patient husband 'twas, who bore*
> *A yamnoy, huge and bulky;*
> *It weighed a dozen pounds or more —*
> *No wonder he was sulky.*

> *And as he ran to catch the car,*
> *More and still more disgusted,*
> *His yamnoy fell — and, with the jar,*
> *Two watermelons busted!*

Yod, *n.* 1. A ban, or restriction; a rule forbidding pleasant things. 2. A place where one must conform to the proprieties.

Yod, *v.* To behave circumspectly, or with conventional deportment.

Yod'der-y, *a.* Stiff, proper, formal; respectable.

Yes, you have to mind your p's and q's in a Christian Endeavor yod, or in the house of your best girl. Why, in some places, there is even a yod on the tango! (See *Ovotch.*)

Don't you love to get into a place where there's a yod on smoking? A temperance yod is not so bad — except that you can never get good food where they sell soft drinks.

Remember that restaurant they started a couple of years ago where evening dress was required? That business-suit yod killed it.

Poor little slangy Lulu, with the henna hair! When she was introduced to Millionaire Willie's mother, she had so many yods on her that she didn't dare squeak!

Remember that low-necked yod your aunt used to have? Why, nowadays, she wears double-décolleté in a trolley-car. No, those sanctimonious old yoddery days of yore are well gone by. Your wife smokes cigarettes now — your daughter's skirts are slit up to the knee. However, there's still a yod on woman suffrage, and we may hold 'em down. (See *Varm.*)

> *There was a yod on swearing at*
>   *The home of Mr. Badd,*
> *So this was how he had to spat,*
>   *When he was good and mad: —*
>
> *" Cognominate that blastoderm!*
>   *You jacitating void,*
> *You go to Heligoland and squirm,*
>   *You lepidopteroid!"*

Yowf, *n.* 1. One whose importance exceeds
his merit. A rich, or influential fool. 2.
Stupidness, combined with authority.

You find the yowf sitting at the Captain's table on ship-
board; and at the speakers' dais at banquets. He is top-
heavy with importance, and soggy with self-esteem.

Among the yowfs present were: The Mayor of the Small
Town; a state senator; the Dock Commissioner; a bank president, two consuls, the Commandant of the Navy Yard, a
police judge, and the Treasurer of the Wild Cat Club. (See
Edicle.)

The yowf is long on dignity, and short on charm; but he
has to be waited on first. The female yowf has a 46 bust
measure, and is important mainly on account of her clothes.

It is always a yowf who gives the reception to visiting
celebrities. He travels all over the world, and somehow,
is able to mingle constantly with people with real brains.
(See *Machizzle.*)

> *The yowf was traveling on a pass —*
> *And he was grand and fat.*
> *A Fourth Vice Presidential ass,*
> *Or something big like that.*

> *I could not bear him; so, one noon,*
> *I pricked him with a pin.*
> *He shrivelled, a collapsed balloon —*
> *Naught but an empty skin!*

Zeech, *n.*   1. A person of too strong individual-
ity. One whose personality dominates.   2.
A monologuist or violent talker.
Zeech'ous, *a.* Lively, but tiresome; exhaust-
ingly original.

The zeech is usually a good talker and a bad conversa-
tionalist; he colors the party, you have to take his tone.   He
may bring in the sunshine but he destroys those subtler half-
lights which give atmosphere.

Curiously, the zeech is a great mixer and yet he will not
mix; things must go his way.   He is dynamic but has nothing in reserve.   (See *Spuzz.*)

There are no surprises in the zeech — you know what he
is going to do and say.   You will laugh, but in the end be
bored.   He makes the party " go," but prevents its being an
occasion.

The zeech is conspicuous, brilliant — but exhausting.

You invite the zeech to dinner, and the first time you are
enthusiastic about him.   By the third, however, your wife
ventures to say, " Oh, let's not have him *this* time! "   (See
Cowcat.)

> *The zeech told stories without end,*
> *The life of all the party.*
> *He made no joke that could offend,*
> *He made us laugh so hearty!*
>
> *But when at last the door was shut,*
> *She said, and hid a yawn,*
> *" Oh, he was so amusing, but*
> *I'm very glad he's gone! "*

Zob′zib, *n.*   An amiable fool, a blunderer.   One
who is kind, but brainless.
Zob′zib, *v.*   To act with misguided zeal.

The zobzib "means well"—but deliver us from our
friends! He comes too early and he stays too late. He is
always in the way. He calls just before dinner, but he will
not sit down and dine with you. He is always "just going."
He is fond of picking out a tune on the piano with one finger.

When a zobzib enters, you just know he is going to break
or tip over something, or spill claret on the table cloth.
He will surely slip on the rug. He is a bull in a china shop,
he is as hilarious as a wet Newfoundland dog. (See *Splooch*.)

The female zobzib gives you advice, "for your own good."
She asks you to buy tickets for church fairs and charity con-
certs.

A zobzib cannot help missing the train, he cannot help for-
getting the theatre tickets. That's why he's a zobzib. (See
Rawp.)

I've often thought I'd like to be a drunkard, so some nice,
sweet zobzib would marry me, to reform me.

> *A zobzib, with a rag and broom*
> *And dust-pan, came today;*
> *She came to tidy up my room,*
> *While I was far away.*

> *She left, and everything I need*
> *Was zobzibbed out of sight —*
> *I can find nothing, but, indeed,*
> *That Zobzib "meant all right!"*